Chakra Magic for Beginners

Identity – Radiance – Shaping – Enjoying

Contact: www.HarryEilenstein.de
Harry.Eilenstein@web.de
Harry Eilenstein at youtube

Production and publishing house: BoD – Books on Demand, Norderstedt

ISBN: 9783754311073

Table of Contents

4

I The Chakra System

From the point of view of a human being, the world consists fundamentally of consciousness and matter. If we want to put it simply, we can say that matter is the outside of the world and consciousness is its inside.

These two sides of the world are firmly connected: One can make the decision in one's consciousness to stand up now and carry it out with one's body. On the other hand, one can perceive with one's body what is happening in the world and then know that in one's consciousness. The consciousness acts on the body and the body acts on the consciousness. So there must be a firm connection between consciousness and matter.

With the senses (eyes, ears, nose, mouth, skin, etc.) one perceives the external world. With the help of telepathy the consciousness perceives the inner world – e.g. the memory images in another person.

With the hands one forms the outer world. With the help of telekinesis also the consciousness is able to act.

This perception by the consciousness (telepathy) and this acting by the consciousness (telekinesis) are often described as processes in the realm of the life force. However, the life force is neither a force nor a substance, but simply a term with which one can describe the "substance" which the consciousness perceives in a direct way (telepathy) and in which it acts in a direct way (telekinesis). The life force is just the border and transition between consciousness and matter as it is seen directly by the consciousness.

This border is found everywhere: All things have a material substance and a consciousness – and therefore also a life force, i.e. the border between both.

This border between consciousness and matter, this transition between consciousness and matter is the area where magic happens: consciousness shapes the material world in a direct way.

This transition in a human being is the life force body: the transition between inside and outside in a human being.

Since both the material body and consciousness have multiple structures, the life force body also has a structure: the chakras are the "organs" of the life force body and the kundalini is the "life force circuit" of the life force body.

Since magic takes place at the transition from consciousness to matter, the chakras should be of great importance in magic.

I 1. Basic Principle

Consciousness tends toward unity and freedom, which can be experienced through telepathy, telekinesis, meditation and magic, among other things.

Matter, on the other hand, tends towards multiplicity and determinacy (causality), which can be seen in the imprinting of the material world by the laws of nature.

What happens now at the transition between the free unity of consciousness and the determined multiplicity of matter? If the consciousness is one and free and the matter is a multiplicity and fixed, then one should expect something third in between, which is different from both.

What one can find there are simple organic-symmetrical structures, which build up more and more complex forms from a simple basic principle. This is the realm of creativity: one freely shapes out of consciousness the "inert" multiplicity of matter … This is magic and also art … and above all the art of living …

(This dual principle of the contrast-complement of free consciousness and determined, "inert" matter, from which the possibility of magic arises, I have presented in detail in my book "Magic Research for Beginners".)

I 1. a)   Fire and light

The simplest way to describe the chakras is their representation as a mixture of power ("fire") and consciousness ("light"):

Root Chakra: 6/6 fire – 0/6 light
=> vitality, instincts, will to live, needs, power

Hara: 5/6 fire – 1/6 light
=> centered power, inner support, steadfastness, rhythm

Solar Plexus: 4/6 fire – 2/6 light
=> directed power, mobility, invigoration, connection

Heart Chakra: 3/6 fire – 3/6 light
=> center, balance, identity, "temple of the soul"

Throat Chakra: 2/6 fire - 4/6 light
=> conscious creation, community, self-expression

Third Eye: 1/6 fire – 5/6 light
=> directed attention, concentration, alignment

Crown chakra: 0/6 fire – 0/6 light
=> awareness, consciousness, presence, perception

I 1. b)   Symmetry

The heart chakra is the "temple of the soul" – consequently, the heart chakra is the center of the chakra system, which is polar-symmetrical:

The Symmetry of the Seven Main Chakras						
Name	*Alignment*	*Quality*	*Symmetry*			
crown chakra		spiritual contact				
third eye	outside	outer orientation				
throat chakra		social self-expression				
heart chakra	center	identity				
solar plexus		physical self-expression				
hara	inside	inner support				
root chakra		physical contact				

I 1. c) Radiance

The symmetrical structure of the seven main chakras shows that they represent a radiating outward from a center.

The identity in the heart chakra becomes the physical self-expression in the solar plexus and the social self-expression in the throat chakra.

The physical self-expression in the solar plexus becomes the inner hold in the hara; the social self-expression in the throat chakra becomes the outer orientation in the third eye.

The inner hold in the hara becomes the physical contact in the root chakra; the outer orientation becomes the mental contact in the crown chakra.

Thus, there is a "three-stage radiance" emanating from the identity in the heart chakra (soul):

> 1st stage: unrestrained self-expression, general desires
> solar plexus and throat chakra

> 2nd stage: structures, concrete desires
> hara and third eye

> 3rd stage: contact, experience
> root chakra and crown chakra

I 2.   Structure

The overall system of the chakras is not only composed of the seven main chakras, but is much more complex. However, its great diversity is symmetrical and derives from a very simple basic principle and is therefore easy to grasp.

I 2. a)   The Three-Step

The basic element is the unfolding in three steps:

      1. the general orientation towards a general goal = the behavior in the world as a whole

      2. the concrete orientation in a concrete situation = the behavior in a certain place

      3. the contact in the here and now = the experiencing of what one has aimed at by the previous two steps

These three steps lead from the identity to the contact with the world:

      The 1st step brings the person closer to the place where he wants to be. Thus, in the 1st step, he is in the public, in the world as a whole.

      By the 2nd step, the person shapes the circumstances in the place where he arrived by the 1st step. He is thus in a "private area" – precisely in the area he has chosen to stay for a while. The proximity to the surroundings is clearly greater here than in the 1st step.

      In the 3rd step, the person does what he is actually concerned with. He is now in the "intimate area". The contact and closeness are very intense here.

It is probably best to illustrate these three steps with a simple example:

1st step: I am hungry.

2nd step: I decide to eat an apple.

3rd step: I eat the apple.

I 2. b)   Three-Step and Five-Step

This three-step can be supplemented by two more points: One is the starting point and the other is the environment. In the chakra system, the starting point is the heart chakra ("temple of the soul") and the environment is the external world (everything except one's own body).

This results in five points:

heart chakra

    solar plexus / throat chakra

    hara / third eye

    root chakra / crown chakra

environment

One can also represent these five points in another way:

The basic structure of the world consists of matter, consciousness and the transition between these two. This is also a three-step process:

1. the free consciousness, which chooses the direction

2. the transition, where an organic structure is found

3. the material world, in which one experiences concrete encounters

Since the chakra system is a representation of transition, the three pairs of chakras

12

that represent the three steps can also be understood as a differentiation of this transition:

Differentiation		
1st step of differentiation	*2nd step of differentiation*	*3rd step of differentiation*
world	consciousness	consciousness (heart chakra)
	transition (life force)	solar plexus / throat chakra
		hara / third eye
		root chakra / crown chakra
	matter	matter (body)

I 2. c)   The seven main chakras

The seven main chakras are a "3+1+3=7", i.e. the heart chakra as center and starting point of the radiance as well as the two triads "solar plexus – hara – root chakra" and "throat chakra – third eye – crown chakra".

I 2. d)   The twelve minor chakras

The heart chakra radiates not only downward to the root chakra and upward to the crown chakra, but also outward through the limbs, that is, through the arms and legs. The three-step is also found in them:

the 1st step in the upper arms and thighs respectively

the 2nd step in the lower arms and lower legs respectively

the 3rd step in the hands and feet respectively

The three chakras in the middle of the two upper arms, the two lower arms and the two hands, as well as in the middle of the two thighs, the two lower legs and the two feet are the twelve minor chakras: "2·2·3=12".

The three-step dynamic is also clearly visible in them:

The upper leg gives the power to walk and determines the general direction (impulse).

The lower leg orientates itself on the spot and selects a certain direction at the place where the person is at the moment (orientation).

The foot sets itself down in the most suitable place (contact).

The upper arm directs itself to where one wants to do something (impulse).

The forearm moves in the chosen place (orientation).

The hand grasps and forms things at that place (contact).

Major Chakras and Minor Chakras			
Area	*Chakra*		
center	heart chakra		
	Three-Step: 1st step	*Three-Step: 2nd step*	*Three-Step: 3rd step*
upper body	throat chakra	third eye	crown chakra
lower body	solar plexus	hara	root chakra
right arm	upper arm minor chakra	forearm minor chakra	hand chakra
left arm	upper arm minor chakra	forearm minor chakra	hand chakra
right leg	thigh minor chakra	lower leg minor chakra	foot chakra
left leg	thigh minor chakra	lower leg minor chakra	foot chakra

I 2. e)   The intermediate chakras

Each major and minor chakra can be considered as the "capital" of a kingdom that is influenced by it. Between each of these kingdoms there is a boundary where the influence of one chakra ends and the influence of the other chakra begins.

At these borders between the "kingdoms" of the individual chakras are the intermediate chakras. They have the character of gates, of guardians and of places of transformation. They are also arranged symmetrically.

The first six intermediate chakras are located between the main chakras:

Wish-fulfillment tree: heart chakra => solar plexus
- Location: at the lower end of the sternum
- Function: transformation of identity (heart chakra) into general physical desires and body impulses (solar plexus)

Thymus intermediate chakra: heart chakra => throat chakra
- Location: at the upper end of the sternum
- Function: transformation of identity (heart chakra) into general social desires and social impulses (throat chakra)

Navel intermediate chakra: solar plexus => hara
- Location: at the navel (nourishment from inside before birth)
- Function: transformation of a general physical desire (solar plexus) into a concrete physical desire (hara)

Palatal intermediate chakra: throat chakra => third eye
- Location: at the palate (food intake from outside after birth)
- Function: transformation of a general social desire (throat chakra) into a concrete social desire (third eye)

Pubic hair intermediate chakra: hara => root chakra
- Location: at the opper end of the pubic hair
- Function: decision to transform the concrete physical desire (hara) into a physical contact (root chakra)

Head hair intermediate chakra: third eye => crown chakra
- Position: at the base of the main hair
- Function: decision to convert the concrete social desire (third eye) into a social contact (crown chakra)

The next six intermediate chakras are located on the arms:

Shoulder joint intermediate chakras: body
                      => upper arm intermediate chakra
- Location: shoulder joint
- Function: decision to take an action that changes the environment

Elbow intermediate chakras: upper arm minor chakra
                 => forearm intermediate chakra
- Position: elbow
- Function: decision to make a movement at the place where the change is to be made

Wrist intermediate chakras: forearm intermediate chakra
                => hand chakra
- Location: Wrist
- Function: decision to take hold of something and transform it

The next six intermediate chakras are located on the legs:

Hip joint intermediate chakras: abdomen
                   => hip joint intermediate chakra
- Location: hip joint
- Function: decision to go to a certain place

Knee intermediate chakras: thigh intermediate chakra
                => lower leg intermediate chakra
- Position: knee
- Function: decision to move to the place where one is at the moment

Ankle intermediate chakras: lower leg intermediate chakra
                => Foot chakra
- Position: ankle
- Function: decision to place the foot at a certain place

Finally, there are two intermediate chakras located below and above the body, respectively:

"Gate to the fire" intermediate chakra: root chakra => "earth".
    - Location: about a hand's width below the root chakra
    - Function: connection to the earth (life force)

"Gate to the light" intermediate chakra: crown chakra => "heaven".
    - Position: about one hand width above the crown chakra
    - Function: connection to heaven, i.e. to unity (God)

I 2. f) The secondary-intermediate chakras

The chakras are connected by the flow of life force, that forms "canals". This flow and thus these canals also has the three-step dynamic:

1st step: the life force rises from the root chakra in the center of the body like the jet of a waterspout fountain ("Kundalini").

2nd Step: The life force unfolds above the crown chakra like the fountain of a waterspout fountain.

3rd Step: The life force flows back down at the outside of the body like the drops of a waterspout fountain to the root chakra ("aura").

At the ascending flow (Kundalini) are the seven main chakras. This life force flow is called "Sushumna" in yoga. It leads like a path through the seven main chakras and through the gates of the intermediate chakras, which separate the "realms" of the seven main chakras.

To the left and right of this main path there are two secondary paths, which in yoga are called "Ida" and "Pingala". Even though these are three parallel paths, they have a different dynamic than the three-step: in the Sushumna is the image of the soul, and in Ida and Pingala are the male and female mirror images of the soul, that is, the whole inner male image and the whole inner female image.

These two "side paths" also pass through the boundary between the "chakra kingdoms". Therefore, in addition to the intermediate chakras, there is one secondary intermediate chakra on the left and another on the right – so to speak, two secondary gates next to the main gate in the border between two chakra kingdoms. At each of the seven main chakras these three paths meet and cross.

These three "life force channels" are also found on the arms and legs – they correspond to the three acupuncture meridians that run along the front and back of the arms and legs. These three "arm lines" and "leg lines" also form three "gates" at each transition from the "kingdom" of one chakra to the next chakra – that is, at the shoulder joint / hip joint, elbow / knee joint, and wrist / ankle joint.

These secondary-intermediate chakras are of lesser importance in magic.

I 2. g) Acupuncture meridians and the like

This is now quite a large number of major chakras, minor chakras, intermediate chakras and secondary intermediate chakras:

    7 main chakras
    12 minor chakras
    20 intermediate chakras
    36 secondary-intermediate chakras

These altogether 75 different chakras correspond in their characteristics to the different body point systems such as the Chinese acupuncture points, the Tibetan Rang Dröl, the Indian Ayurveda points etc. with a very few exceptions.

(A detailed description and a complete comparison may be found in my book "The Chakra System with the Minor Chakras").

I 2. h) Chakras, kshetrams and aura points

Now there is one last three-step in the chakra system, which is known mainly from traditional Indian medicine, but also, for example, from the methods of the Yaqui shamans in Central America.

Each chakra appears in three forms:

1. inside the body: "chakra".

2. on the surface of the body on the front and the back: "kshetram".

3. on the surface of the life force body, i.e. about an arm's length from the surface of the body on the front and the back: "aura point"

I 3. Chakras and Consciousness

Consciousness and chakras are two different things: Consciousness is one of the two poles of the world (the other is matter) – chakras are structures at the transition between consciousness to matter. Therefore, in a sense, the chakras reflect both consciousness and matter.

The heart chakra and the three pairs of chakras correspond to the four forms of consciousness. From the consciousness side, they are characterized by having consciousness – from the matter side, they are characterized by having different contents.

The four kinds of consciousness can be defined simply by the number of contents of consciousness in them:

the chakras and the types of consciousness		
Chakra	*Type of consciousness*	*Contents of consciousness*
heart chakra	deep sleep consciousness	without contents
throat chakra / solar plexus	subconscious mind	all contents
third eye / hara	waking consciousness	the contents needed in the situation
crown chakra / root chakra	ecstasy	one content

I 3. a)   The house of consciousness

This overview becomes more vivid when described pictorially:

Deep sleep consciousness is consciousness itself without any content. It is the silence that can be found in meditation: a consciousness that is only aware of itself.

This consciousness is like an empty house: full of possibilities, but empty.

The deep sleep consciousness is the silence in the heart chakra, which is the source of all fullness – the central chakra.

The subconscious mind is the totality of all the contents of the conscious mind, that is, all perceptions and all memories – including the feelings that may be associated with them.

The subconscious is like a (well-ordered) archive in which everything that one has ever experienced can be found.

The subconscious consists of the general and all-encompassing desires and impulses in the solar plexus below the heart chakra and in the throat chakra above the heart chakra – the two inner main chakras.

The waking consciousness contains the contents that one needs in the momentary situation in order to be able to decide sensibly for an action. The subconscious either sends these contents to the waking consciousness on its own or the waking consciousness has to get them, i.e. consciously remember them.

The waking consciousness is like an office in the house, where the current processes are regulated. From the office there is a passage to the archive, through which the currently needed information reaches the waking consciousness.

The waking consciousness is in the inner support of the hara and in the orientation in the world of the third eye – the two middle main chakras.

The state of ecstasy contains only one content. This happens when this one content is extremely important. Therefore, the single-mindedness of ecstasy arises from fear, pain, pleasure or meditation.

Ecstasy may be thought of as a desk lamp on the desk in the office, sometimes turned on to highlight a single thing with a bright spotlight.

The state of ecstasy arises from physical or mental contact with the world in the root chakra or in the crown chakra – the two outer main chakras.

All well-grounded impulses of the human being pass through this series of consciousnesses:

In the beginning there is identity: heart chakra.

From it, impulses and needs generally arise in the subconscious: solar plexus and throat chakra.

In the waking consciousness they become concrete goals and strategies: hara and third eye.

In the ecstatic state, a single thing is experienced in the here and now: root chakra and crown chakra.

The fifth element is the world outside one's own body, which is touched, changed and experienced by this process.

I 3. b)   The principle of octaves

The four states of consciousness can be recognized by an EEG – each state of consciousness has a certain frequency:

The Symmetry of the Seven Main Chakras							
Name	*Type of consciousness*	*EEG frequency*		*Symmetry*			
crown chakra	state of ecstasy	16 – 32 Hz	Ø 24Hz				
third eye	waking consciousness	8 – 16 Hz	Ø 12Hz				
throat chakra	subconsciousness	4 – 8 Hz	Ø 6Hz				
heart chakra	deep sleep consciousness	2 – 4 Hz	Ø 3Hz				
solar plexus	subconscious mind	4 – 8 Hz	Ø 6Hz				
hara	waking consciousness	8 – 16 Hz	Ø 12Hz				
root chakra	state of ecstasy	16 – 32 Hz	Ø 24Hz				

This overview clearly shows that the four different states of consciousness each has twice the frequency as the state of consciousness below it:

The subconsciousness has twice the frequency of the deep sleep.

The waking has twice the frequency of the subconscious.

The ecstasy has a frequency twice as high as the waking consciousness.

In musical terms, the deep sleep consciousness is the keynote, the subconsciousness is the next higher octave of that keynote, the waking consciousness is the second higher octave of that keynote, and the ecstasy state is the third higher octave of the keynote.

The consciousness sings in a four-part chorus …

The way from the heart chakra through the six other main chakras to the outside is therefore also a narrowing down to a selected content of consciousness.

This decision in three steps for a certain thing in the world should therefore also be an essential element in magic: decided one-pointedness …

I 3. c) Meditation

The various forms of meditation consist of coordinating the waking consciousness with one of the other states of consciousness. The waking consciousness is always present because meditation is a conscious activity.

waking consciousness + subconsciousness   = dream journey
waking consciousness + deep sleep consciousness   = silent meditation
waking consciousness + ecstasy state   = one-pointedness

There are also complex meditations that combine more than two forms of consciousness like mandala-meditations and mandala-rituals.

The coordination of the rhythms of consciousness in meditation		
uncoordinated rhythm (normal consciousness)		
deep sleep		
dream		
waking		
ecstasy		
coordinated rhythm (meditation)		
deep sleep		
dream		
waking		
ecstasy		

I 3. d)   The city of consciousness

There is more than one human being and the consciousnesses of these people are not isolated from each other – as the many manifestations of telepathy impressively show.

This means that there is not only a "house of consciousness", but also a "city of consciousness". The houses in this city are connected with each other on all levels:

The "City of Consciousness"	
the "House of Consciousness"	*the "City of Consciousness"*
deep sleep consciousness	all-embracing consciousness ("God")
subconsciousness	collective subconsciousness (magic)
waking consciousness	collective planning (politics etc.)
ecstasy	collective acting (sex, fear etc.)
(body)	(world)

In this "city of consciousness" also magic takes place – starting from a simple telepathy up to miracles like materializations. The chakras are the places where something is created; they are the places where a person's identity comes out of consciousness into the material world and shapes it.

The six outer chakras with their different states of consciousness are the gateways between the pure consciousness (without content) in the heart chakra in one's own body and the material world in general.

I 4.   Disturbances

In every complex system there can be disturbances – this is not different with the chakra system. Therefore, if one wants to use the chakras in magic, it is useful to know their possible disturbances.

I 4. a)   Disturbances of the heart chakra

The identity in the heart chakra is always preserved – however, it can radiate more or less well outward to the other chakras. Since the heart chakra corresponds to the inner silence, that is, to the "consciousness without consciousness contents", this "empty space" is not influenced by the consciousness contents within in the mind of a person.

Consciousness as such is always there – there may only different things take place in it. However, this "drama of the contents of consciousness" takes place in the six main outer chakras, all of which contain contents of consciousness:

- Solar plexus and throat chakra: all contents (subconsciousness).

- Hara and third eye: the contents that are important in the momentary situation (waking consciousness)

- Root chakra and crown chakra: a single content (ecstatic state).

I 4. b)   Disturbances of the solar plexus

The healthy state of the solar plexus is the unhindered physical self-expression. Subjectively, this is perceived as self-love.

When life force accumulates here, i.e. when this chakra becomes dominant, the "star" arises, which wants to attract all attention to itself.

A life force congestion in this chakra causes a life force deficiency in its opposite pole, i.e. in the throat chakra.

I 4. c) Disturbances of the throat chakra

The healthy state of the throat chakra is unhindered social self-expression. Subjectively, this is perceived as self-love.

When life force accumulates here, that is, when this chakra becomes dominant, the "fan" arises who directs all his attention to someone else.

A life force congestion in this chakra causes a life force deficiency in its opposite pole, i.e. in the solar plexus.

I 4. d) Disturbances of the hara

The healthy state of the hara is the unimpeded physical living. Subjectively, this is perceived as strength.

If life force accumulates here, i.e. if this chakra becomes dominant, the "perpetrator" arises, who ruthlessly asserts himself against all others.

A life force congestion in this chakra causes a life force deficiency in its opposite pole, i.e. in the third eye.

I 4. e) Disturbances of the third eye

The healthy state of the Third Eye is the unimpeded social living. Subjectively, this is perceived as strength.

When life force accumulates here, that is, when this chakra becomes dominant, the "victim" arises who cannot defend himself against anyone.

A life force congestion in this chakra causes a life force deficiency in its opposite pole, i.e. in the hara.

I 4. f) Disturbances of the root chakra

The healthy state of the root chakra is unhindered physical contact. Subjectively, this is perceived as abundance.

If life force accumulates here, i.e. if this chakra becomes dominant, the "addict" arises who can never get enough.

A life force congestion in this chakra causes a life force deficiency in its opposite pole, i.e. in the crown chakra.

I 4. g)   Disorders of the crown chakra

The healthy state of the crown chakra is unhindered social contact. Subjectively, this is perceived as abundance.

When life force accumulates here, that is, when this chakra becomes dominant, the "ascetic" arises who renounces everything.

A life force congestion in this chakra causes a life force deficiency in its opposite pole, i.e. in the root chakra.

I 4. h)   Overview

These six possible deviations from the " middle path", i.e. these six aberrations, can be summarized in an overview:

Possible Disturbances in the Six Outer Main Chakras				
pair of chakras	*chakras*	*whole state*	*deviations*	
			"too loud" (life force congestion in one of the three lower chakras)	*"too quiet"* (life force congestion in one of the three upper chakras)
1st pair	solar plexus	self-love	star	
	throat chakra			fan
2nd pair	hara	strength	perpetrator	
	third eye			victim
3rd pair	root chakra	abundance	addict	
	crown chakra			ascetic

The three forms of the wholesome state contain all the "pleasant feelings" and the six deviations that arise from the three polarizations contain all the "unpleasant feelings".

For example, when strength meets an obstacle that hinders one's actions, anger arises. If the anger achieves nothing, it can either be further increased, which then gives rise to the hatred and cruelty of the perpetrator, or it can be directed inward, which then gives rise to the sadness and depression of the victim. Therefore, healing both hatred (perpetrator) and sadness (victim) leads back to the "whole strength" via the original anger.

(I have presented these connections in detail in my book "Feelings and Their Transformations".)

These connections between the chakras and the feelings are interesting in relation to the subject of this book only because they show how fundamentally important the chakras and their states (whole or polarized) are for our lives. The importance of the chakras and their state goes far beyond magic and concerns our daily living.

I 5. Applications in Magic

The chakras are used partly consciously, but mostly rather unconsciously also in magic. Since magic is the creative use of the freedom of consciousness in its effect on "inert" matter, this is not to be expected otherwise.

A systematic use of the chakras is not common in magic – they are rather sometimes considered incidentally.

In India, where the awakening of the chakras is a central part of yoga, the chakras appear as elements of the Yoga system because of their importance for meditation, and are therefore also considered systematically. Magic in Yoga is but a side effect, which is usually even undesirable. The magical abilities acquired by meditation are called "siddhis" and are often considered merely an undesirable interference with meditation. "Siddhi" simply means "ability."

A synthesis of meditation and magic, in which both are equally contained, has not yet been developed. The present book is, among other things, an attempt to describe both as an organic unity.

I 5. a) The heart chakra in magic

Magic

The heart chakra is the "temple of the soul". Therefore, the heart chakra is an important chakra in "High Magic", which is, among other things, also about self-knowledge. Here one finds one's own identity. One's own soul appears to oneself, as long as one has not yet recognized it as one's own center, as one's own guardian spirit or guardian angel.

The heart chakra is sometimes associated with a golden chalice – the Grail. This is a symbol of devotion to one's own soul.

Chakra qualitites

The awakening of the heart chakra leads to the recognition of oneself and the knowledge of one's own psyche. This leads to the dissolution of all contradictions and a deep self-affirmation as well as an inner freedom and an unshakable optimism based on this experience. Since one rests in oneself, one no longer clings to anything. Noticeable are the very fine sense of touch and the frequent enjoyment of sounds. Self-awareness often leads to creative impulses.

Siddhis

The magical siddhis of the heart chakra include telepathy and also the perception of the past and future, and telekinesis. One can perceive other people's states of mind very accurately. There is also a tendency to astral travel as well as the ability to heal by touch or even just well-wishing.

Sleep

People in whom the heart chakra is the most active of all the chakras often sleep for only 4-6 hours, usually lying on their left side.

I 5. b)   The solar plexus in magic

Magic

The solar plexus organizes the flows of life force in one's body. Therefore, the life force connections to other people are also found here, which can be perceived as milky white life force threads with a slight blue shimmer. They are also called "silver cords". They are partly desirable, e.g. between a mother and her child, because the mother can by this telepathically perceive when her child is in danger, and partly undesirable, because life force vampirism can be practiced by them.

Unwanted silver cords can be cut imaginatively with a knife directly above one's own solar plexus. One should then paint a protective sign (pentagram, cross, etc.) on one's own solar plexus – either imaginatively or with dragon's blood (ground resin from the dragon tree). The now open end of the cut silver cord, which is still attached to the other person, should be given to Mother Earth, so that this free end does not attach itself again to the same person or to someone else. The other person to whom this silver cord led need not be present during this silver cord cutting, of course.

Chakra Qualities

During the awakening of the solar plexus, there sometimes arises a recognition of one's connectedness with all beings by silver cords, or also a recognition of the lack of boundaries of consciousness. The psyche begins to heal as one awakens the solar plexus and one develops a deeper understanding of one's own body and the life force flowing within it. The unfolding of compassion and benevolence also occurs. This leads altogether to a constant happiness.

Siddhis

Since the solar plexus represents the life-force flows in the body, the awakening of the solar plexus leads to vigorous health and great vitality, as well as conspicuous longevity. One discovers within oneself the power to create and destroy – one learns to direct one's own life force. This also leads to fearlessness and a much improved ability to defend oneself. As one can increasingly direct one's own power, which is symbolically fire, one loses any fear of fire (firewalking). More prominent siddhis are discovering remedies and finding hidden treasures.

Sleep

People in whom the solar plexus is most active of all the chakras usually sleep 6-8 hours a night, lying on their backs. This is the most common condition in adults.

I 5. c)   The throat chakra in magic

Magic

The throat chakra is used for communication and coordination. It is the chakra of social self-expression: one shows others who one is and ideally does not allow oneself to be deterred from remaining true to oneself.

Chakra qualities

The throat chakra enables one to perceive the thoughts and feelings of others – it is the chakra by which one shows oneself to others and by which one sees others.

An important point is that the mind stops trying to direct everything – it becomes again the "helper of the heart". Nevertheless, one has a need to know and to be known, and in this context one stops repressing things. In doing so, one develops serenity, seriousness, purity and non-attachment. In addition, one stops judging things – although one certainly has a direction and an opinion.

One becomes a careful researcher, a good listener, a talented teacher, a skillful writer, a gifted speaker, and has great knowledge.

One works without sticking to the fruits. In "Conversations with God" it is said in this regard that one should strive with all intensity for what one wants to achieve, but always remain independent of whether one achieves it or not. This intensity, alignment and at the same time independence is an essential quality of both the solar plexus and the throat chakra.

Siddhis

The awakening of the throat chakra, like the solar plexus, promotes the strength of the body and therefore leads to rejuvenation and, so to speak, to "eternal youth." The fearlessness that is often observed in an intact throat chakra is also related to this awakening power.

One perceives the past, the present and the future. One can also effortlessly understand other world views and also dreams of other people.

The awakening of the throat chakra significantly reduces the feelings of hunger and thirst.

Overall, people with an active throat chakra tend to have the Taoist attitude of "Relax into the here and now." and "Eat when you are hungry; sleep when you are tired."

Sleep

If the throat chakra is the most active of all the chakras, 4-6 hours of sleep per night is typical.

I 5. d)   The hara in magic

Magic

The hara is the central element in combat magic, as it is associated with steadfastness and dominance – in extreme cases, a life force congestion in the hara gives rise to the perpetrator/sadist type.

An intact hara is also conducive to the practice of hypnosis.

Chakra qualities

The awakening of the hara leads to greater self-confidence and steadfastness and thus indirectly to greater self-esteem. This can also lead to fairness and chivalry towards others.

The inner effect is the emergence of a deep peace. However, this inner peace is not something static, but something flowing – the inner support is a rhythm, a staying in the flow. This is true for any sport, for sex, for dance, for fighting and also for all other forms of movement.

The healing of the hara leads to a reduction of lust, greed and hatred – the extreme image of the "doer" dissolves and a person who rests in his strength emerges.

The inner support also leads to a better understanding of one's own body. Often the sense of taste also becomes more sensitive.

Siddhis

By the awakening of the hara, intuitive knowledge and intuitive speech emerge – both telepathy and telekinesis become stronger. Even more noticeable is the spontaneous fulfillment of wishes – which is also based on telepathy/telekinesis.

There are also reports of a dissolution of the fear of water – because one no longer needs an outer support, but has found an inner support in the hara?

If you look in a dream journey at the state of consciousness of Jesus while he walked over the water of the Sea of Galilee, you will also find this perfect inner security, in which there is not the slightest hint of doubt about what you are doing: the inner support of the hara.

Sleep

In people in whom the hara is the most active chakra, 8-10 hours of sleep in the fetal position is common.

I 5. e)   The third eye in magic

Magic

The Third Eye is the chakra of concentration, perception, empathy, clairvoyance (optical perception of the life force as a milky white glow) and also imagination, which is the active counterpart of passive clairvoyance.

Since imagination is an essential element in magic, the third eye is well developed in many magicians – but they also need a well-developed hara to have a formative effect on their environment.

The third eye is of course also the central chakra for the seers – although they do not necessarily need a strong hara, since they only perceive, but do not imprint.

Chakra qualities

By awakening the third eye, independence and a freedom from limitations emerge, and thus ultimately a self-designed way of life.

Since all things are always seen as part of the whole, constant change no longer causes suffering – and feelings of lack, weakness and worthlessness gradually calm down.

One understands causality increasingly better – and also karma, if one believes that to be real.

One experiences samadhi ("non-duality") and probably develops the inclination to live alone as a yogi or the like.

Siddhis

By the third eye, one can intuit things, distinguish truth from error and lies, and perceive the past and the future. This ability as well as the seeing of the aura of people and things together result in a talent in using oracles.

A striking feature of the active third eye, as with the hara, is that resolutions are immediately followed by the result – spontaneous wish fulfillment.

"Aum" is the best mantra for this chakra.

Sleep

When the third eye is the most active chakra in a person, often only 2 hours of sleep are needed per night.

I 5. f)   The root chakra in magic

Magic

In magic, the root chakra is mainly used for awakening the kundalini and for sexual magic (charging talismans by sex, among other things).

Rather unknown, but extremely helpful is the connecting of the root chakra by an imagined life force light thread ("silver cord") to the glowing iron-nickel core in the center of the earth, which is the root chakra of the earth. This is an easy way to charge oneself with power.

Chakra Qualities

By awakening the root chakra, many suppressed feelings become conscious, which sometimes leads to aggression and fear – possibly also to feelings of lack. In such a phase a lot of security, sleep and food is needed – typical needs when there is a lack of abundance.

When the root chakra has been healed, the lack is replaced by abundance – and the addict is replaced by the "sated child". As a result, there is again a security and inner purity, and one becomes balanced and joyful. Since the mind no longer has to eliminate an unbearable condition, the mind can also shrink back to its normal size and no longer needs to take on tasks for which it is not suited.

A side effect of this recovery of inner fullness is a soft and at the same time powerful voice.

An increase in the sense of smell has also been observed – it is one of the oldest sense organs developed early in evolution.

Siddhis

By awakening the life force in the root chakra, there is also an unusual physical power, whereby one attains the charisma of a king.

Since the life force in the root chakra can flow freely again, abundance arises again, obstacles dissolve, and one succeeds easily – every thought seems to come true effortlessly. In addition, one is protected from diseases.

One possibly remembers past lives. Moreover, telepathy of any kind becomes easier and easier.

One seems to become a "friend of the earth" – for example, one almost always remains unharmed in falls.

The awakening of the root chakra also seems to promote the learning of astral travel.

Another phenomenon is the "frog-hopping siddhi," which is a precursor to levitation. In this siddhi, while sitting in the lotus position, the legs make involuntary movements that cause one to make small jumps.

Sleep

When this chakra is most active in a person, 10-12 hours of sleep are usually needed. Most of the time the person lies on his belly.

I 5. g) The crown chakra in magic

Magic

The crown chakra is the connection to "above". Therefore, devotion, prayer and invocations (identification with a deity) belong to this chakra.

Chakra Qualities

By the awakening of the crown chakra, one can experience the oneness behind the multiplicity. One becomes focused and unified – oneness, subject, object, and experience become one; the delineation of consciousness dissolves. In the Indian tradition, this state is called "I am that" ("Tat twam asi" or "Aham Bramhasmin"). In the Jewish Kabbalah, this is called "I am who I am." ("Eheieh").

One aspect of this process is that the inner man and woman unite with each other, allowing one again to perceive one's own soul – the life force flows from Ida and Pingala into the Sushumna. This is a central aspect of Yoga. On the mythological level, this is the union of Shiva and Shakti.

By this one attains wisdom, serenity and bliss.

Siddhis

One perceives spirits, deities, and the will of deities, and one attains a vision of one's guru or deity.

One has attained all the siddhis, but does not feel the need to use them – except when it feels right, for example, in a healing.

Sleep

When this chakra is fully awakened, one no longer needs sleep – the "instrument" always remains tuned and one no longer needs sleep to tune one's instrument again.

I 5. h)   The hand chakras in magic

The hand chakras are used for telepathic perception and life force transmission for healing and blessings. One can also receive life force by the hand chakras, e.g. from the sun or the moon, by holding the palms of the hands towards the sun or the moon.

These two chakras a quite easy to perceive, when one directs the palms to the sun or the moon and obserces the feelings in one's hands.

I 5. i)   The foot chakras in magic

With the help of the foot chakras one can ground oneself, i.e. establish a connection to the earth and receive life force from it. The easiest way to do this is to stand bare-foot on the earth.

I 5. j)   Overview of "sleep and chakras"

Some more research would be useful – especially on the sleep postures.

Sleep and Chakras		
dominant chakra	*Sleep duration*	*Sleep posture*
crown chakra	0 hours	-
third eye	2 hours	?
throat chakra	4 – 6 hours	?
heart chakra	4 – 6 hours	on the left side
solar plexus	6 – 8 hours	on the back
hara	8 – 10 hours	in the fetal position
root chakra	10 – 12 hours	?

I 6. The Awakening of the Chakras

There are general methods that can be applied to all chakras, as well as specific methods that can be applied to a pair of chakras or even to a single chakra.

The general method is to imagine directing life force into the chakra in question while inhaling and to let this life force glow or light up there while exhaling.

When inhaling, one speaks inwardly either the name of the chakra or of a deity whom one asks for help, and when exhaling the name of the quality of this chakra – e.g. "Shiva – Fire" in the root chakra. One can also simply speak "fire" internally both while inhaling and exhaling.

In doing so, one imagines either the chakra itself or a symbol within it – e.g. fire in the root chakra.

This meditation should be filled with feeling – with the longing to awaken this chakra and to fill oneself with its quality.

With the help of the different types of consciousness that belong to the heart chakra and the three pairs of chakras, one can form more specific meditations that awaken these chakras – the waking consciousness is always present, since meditating is a conscious process:

> heart chakra: deep sleep consciousness (and waking consciousness).
>   = Silence meditation
>
> solar plexus / throat chakra: (waking consciousness and subconsciousness)
>   = dream journeys, imaginations
>
> hara / third eye: waking consciousness
>   = clarity, sincerity, directness; showing oneself as one is
>
> root chakra / crown chakra: ecstatic state (and waking consciousness)
>   = one-pointedness, tantra, being in the here and now

For the individual chakras there are also various exercises in Hatha-Yoga, which consist of certain postures, movements, breathing exercises, mantras, etc.

Now this is only a general overview – the individual method to awaken one's own chakras will almost always contain a variety of aids and will also almost never follow a 'straight path', but a path with many mountains, valleys, potholes, unexpected helps, sudden realizations, trying out new things and much more …

I 7.   The Three-Step in Magic

So far, mainly the chakras have been described, which are characterized by the three-step, but not yet the three-step in magic. This has the same dynamics in magic as in the chakras, since the chakras are the path by which the magical-creative impulses come into the world from the consciousness.

The beginning is in the heart chakra, in the "I am." This is the source of every magically effective action.
This happens in the stillness of deep sleep consciousness.

The first step is uninhibited self-expression: identity becomes a feeling, a general desire, an impulse – one wants to express and experience something … ultimately, one always wants to experience oneself.
This happens in the self-love of the subconsciousness.

The second step is the concretization of the general desire: one chooses in the world a certain place, a time, a person, in order to experience what is desired – one decides, plans, does and fights for what one wants to achieve.
This is done in the strength of the waking consciousness.

The third step is the actual experiencing: One is completely in the here and now and perceives what is, one-pointedly, with all the senses.
This happens in the fullness of the ecstatic state.

The "beginning point" is ultimately also the most important: If you do not rest in yourself and act from your heart, you only create things that you did not really want to have …

The first and the second step are well known from magic: The first step is concentration, that is, unrestrained focus on a goal; the second step is using a method, an analogy, a structure. The second step must root in the first step – otherwise that what you do is like a soulless text read from a prepared script and not like words filled with feelings, that come straight from the heart.

The third step is to experience the result of the magical action – one must also be able to accept and enjoy the fruits, because otherwise the whole thing ultimately has no value.

These three steps between the heart chakra and the world will be considered in more detail in the next chapter.

II Structure and Occurrence of the Three-Step

In order to effectively apply the three-step of the chakras in magic, it is helpful to describe the three qualities of this three-step (plus its source in the heart chakra) as deeply, precisely and vividly as possible. To do this, it is necessary to look at this three-step in a variety of ways, and to gather and combine the insights one finds in the process.

II 1.   The Three-Step

One can find the three-step in the most different areas. The examples given in the following are arranged in the seven subject areas from which they originate: Physics – Psychology – History – Economy – Everyday Life – Astrology – Magic.

– Physics –

II 1. a)   The three basic forces

There are three basic forces, which are clearly different in their nature. Various other forces are derived from them, which are, however, in their actual nature more complex manifestations of these three forces.

Gravitation is the oldest, simplest and weakest of the three basic forces. It is unipolar, i.e. it works between everything – between every matter and every energy. It pulls everything together. It is the weakest of the three forces.
It corresponds to 'phase 1', which is the unrestrained, unrestricted, all-encompassing self-expression.

The electromagnetic force is the second oldest of the three basic forces and from its strength the middle one of the three forces. It is two-polar (+ and -) and works only between particles which have an electric charge. Two particles that have an equal charge, one of which is "+" and the other "-", are together neutral. They attract each other when the charge is different and they repel each other when their charge is the same.

41

It corresponds to 'Phase 2', where structures, attractions and repulsions occur, i.e. a selection is made and different reactions occur.

Each particle with an electromagnetic charge reacts also to gravity.

The color force or strong interaction is the third oldest and strongest of the three basic forces and occurs only in the atomic nucleus. It is three-polar ("red", "yellow", "blue") and acts only between particles that have a "color charge". Three particles which have an equal charge, which is "red" for one particle, "yellow" for one and "blue" for the third, are together neutral ("white"). This force has no color, of course, but has only been so named because the simile to the mixture of the three primary colors, which yield "white", has been so obvious.

It corresponds to the 'phase 3', in which everything is pulled together and unified – just as also the color force binds three particles firmly together.

Each particle with a "color charge" reacts also to the electromagnetic force and to the gravitation.

Summary

Phase 1: The gravitation is unipolar, all-embracing and unrestricted – "uninhibited".

Phase 2: The electromagnetic force is two-polar and creates both bondings and opposite-repulsions.

Phase 3: The color force is three-polar and pulls everything together to one point – one-directionality.

=> The three phases have clearly different properties.

II 1. b)   The three sizes of the elementary particles

The material world consists of four basic building blocks: the up-quark, the down-quark, the electron and the neutrino. The protons and the neutrons are composed of three quarks each. The atoms consist of these two kinds of quarks and the electrons.

Property of the four basic elementary particles			
Particle	*Property*		
	mass (gravitation)	*electromagnetic charge*	*color charge*
up-quark	x	x	x
down-quark	x	x	x
electron	x	x	
neutrino	x		

These four particles appear in three different sizes, of which only the smallest size is stable. The largest form decays to the second largest and this in turn decays to the smallest.

These three sizes correspond to the three-step.

the 12 basic elementary particles			
	1st family *normal particles* *(phase 1)*	*2nd family* *heavy particles* *(phase 2)*	*3rd family* *very heavy particles* *(phase 3)*
quark 1	"up"-quark	„charm"-quark	„truth"-quark
quark 2	„down"- quark	„strange"- quark	„beauty"- quark
leptons	electron	muon	tauon
neutrinos	electron neutrino	muon neutrino	tauon neutrino

Summary

Phase 1: It is the most stable form.
Phase 2: It is the second most stable form.
Phase 3: It is the third most stable form.

=> All particles have the tendency to return to 'phase 1'.

43

II 1. c)   The solar wind

The solar wind is the radiation emitted by the Sun – not only the light itself, but also the particles ejected by it into space (mainly protons and electrons). The solar wind is a part of the space surrounding the sun.

The center is the radiating <u>sun</u>.
It corresponds to the radiant heart chakra.

Around the sun is an area entirely characterized by the photons (light) emitted by the sun and the ions (electrically charged particles) emitted by it. In this area all matter ("stardust") has been blown away to the outside by this <u>"solar wind"</u>.
This area around the sun, which is completely shaped by the sun, corresponds to the unrestricted physical self-expression of the solar plexus and the unrestricted social self-expression of the throat chakra.

The solar wind pushes all small-grained matter ("stardust") in its surrounding space outward and away from the sun on all sides like a snow pusher. This forms a kind of wall in front of the solar wind, consisting of the stardust and ions emitted by the sun. It is called the <u>"shock front"</u>. The total mass of this "envelope" is approximately equal to the mass of the Earth, but it consists only of finely divided dust.
This envelope around the area around the sun, which is shaped by the solar wind, corresponds to the two form chakras: The hara gives one a firm inner support and the third eye gives one an orientation in the whole surrounding space.

The shock front gradually moves further and further outward away from the sun, since the solar wind constantly blows against this shock front from within and constantly gives it new thrust. Thus the area shaped by the solar wind becomes ever larger around the sun. This expanding shock front, which is a spherical shell of stardust and solar ions, moves through the stardust in space like a ship in water. This creates a <u>"bow wave"</u> of stardust in front of the shock front.
This "bow wave" corresponds to the two outer chakras, which, like the bow wave, make contact with the environment: The root chakra is the physical contact and the crown chakra is the spiritual contact.

Outside this area, which is characterized by the sun, is the <u>outer space</u> with the stardust (tiny particles of matter) in it.

This area corresponds to the outer world.

These three spaces around the sun (solar wind space, shock front, bow wave) correspond to the qualities of the three pairs of chakras. The sun itself corresponds to the heart chakra.

But the analogy between the solar system and the chakra system does not end there:

> The sun contains ions, electrically charged particles. When an electric charge moves (as in the case of the sun by its rotation), a magnetic field is created. The magnetic field is always at right angles to the direction of motion of the electric charge. Because of the rotation of the star, planet or galaxy this results in two rays emerging from the two poles. They are two beams because there are both positively and negatively charged ions and the magnetic fields created by their motion point in opposite directions. This is also how the magnetic north pole and the magnetic south pole of the Earth are created, which allow the use of a compass. These two magnetic jets coming out of the poles of the sun are called "jets".
>
> These two "jets" are found in the life force body as the path of the Kundalini, which rises from the lower chakra to the highest chakra. This path ("life force channel") is called "Sushumna" in yoga.

At the points where this "jet" flies from the two poles of the sun through the three areas, vortices are formed.

These "vortices" at the points where the two jets fly through the three areas of the sun's circumference correspond to the three chakras above the heart chakra and below the heart chakra. The vortex at the jets corresponds to the circular motion of the chakras.

The magnetic jets, in turn, affect the ions around them and accelerate them outward away from the sun. Since these ions usually already have a motion of their own, they do not fly away outward in a straight line in the jets themselves, but assume an outwardly moving spiral path around the jet. Thereby, the negatively charged ions rotate in a spiral whose direction of spiral rotation is opposite to the spiral of the positively charged ions.

In yoga, these two spirals are found as the two "life force channels" Ida and Pingala. Since these spiral movements can only be reproduced two-dimensionally on the drawings (in the yoga scriptures), they appear as two symmetrical serpentine lines (as also on the staff of Hermes). In Ida and Pingala the inner female-image and the inner male-image can be found, which corresponds to the opposite charge of the ions in the two spirals. In the central "life force channel", which is called "Sushumna" in yoga, is the gender-independent self-image of the human being (image of the soul).

In the sun, there is a <u>convection current</u>: in the center, matter is heated by the nuclear fusion that takes place there, rises upward like the water jet of a fountain, spreads out on the surface like the fountain of a fountain, cools down there, and then sinks down again like the drops of a fountain.

In the life force body, there is also a convection current: from the root chakra, the life force rises upward like the water jet of a fountain ("awakened Kundalini"), spreads out like the fountain of a fountain on the surface (surface of the aura), and then sinks back down to the root chakra like the drops of a fountain.

The similarity between the two systems becomes even clearer when represented graphically:

The Solar System and the Chakra System

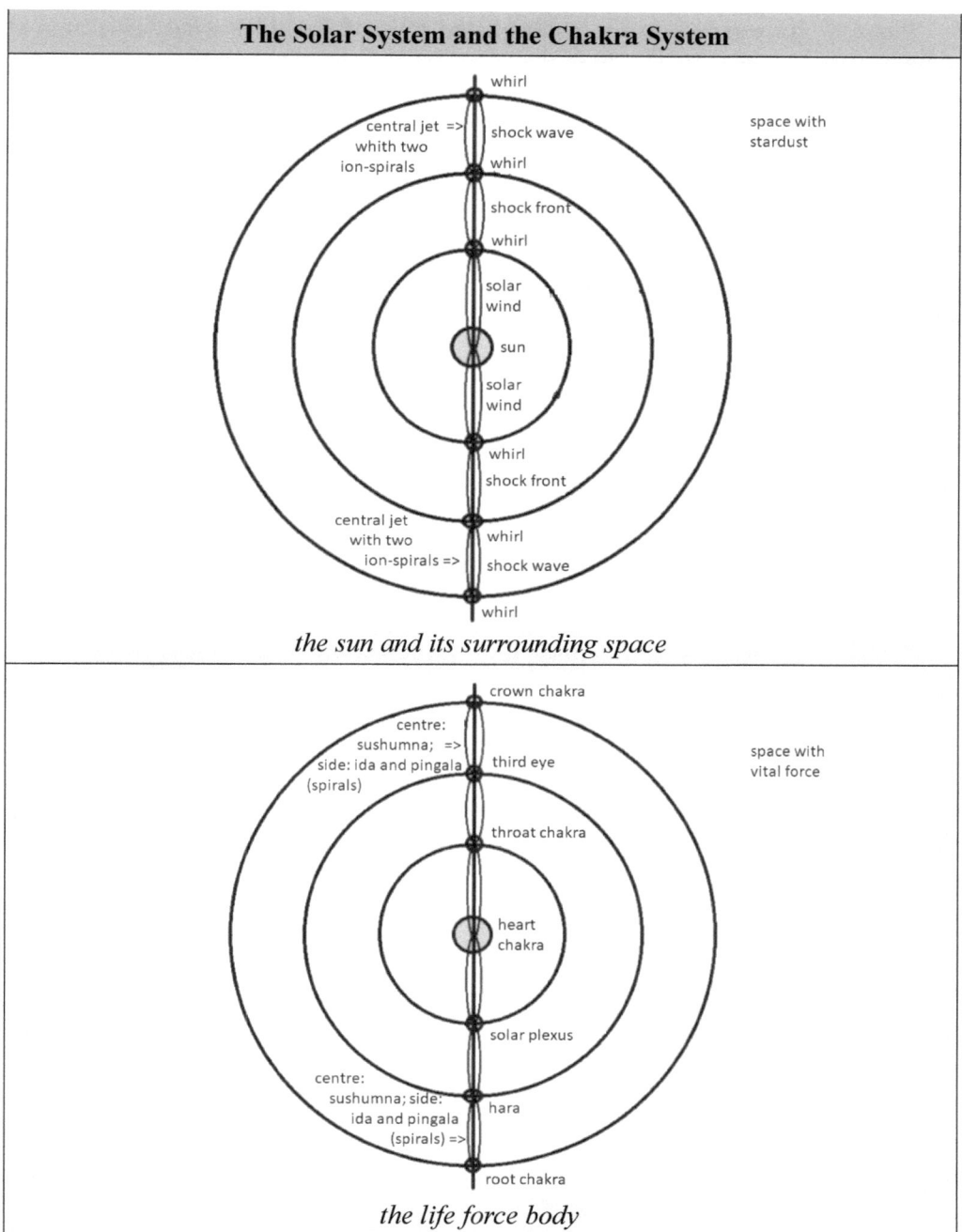

the sun and its surrounding space

the life force body

'Phase 1' corresponds to the unobstructed rays of the solar wind. This area is completely dominated by the sun or the heart chakra ('sun chakra').

'Phase 2' corresponds to the shock front where inner (solar wind) and outer (stardust) meet.

'Phase 3' corresponds to the bow wave, which is an impulse wave moving from the shock front into the surrounding space.

Summary

Phase 1: complete imprinting by the centre = inside-determined
Phase 2: partial imprinting by the centre = inside- and outside-determined
Phase 3: partial imprinting by the centre = inside-influence in outside-area

=> The extent of imprinting decreases from inside (phase 1) to outside (phase 3).

– Psychology –

II 1. d) Subconsciousness, waking consciousness and ecstasy

In the psyche there are the four states of consciousness corresponding to the heart chakra source and the three phases:

Source: the deep sleep consciousness, which exists completely independently of its contents

Phase 1: the subconscious mind, in which all contents are equal and are therefore a complete picture

Phase 2: the waking consciousness, in which the contents important for the momentary situation are located

Phase 3: the ecstasy consciousness, in which only the one most important content is located.

Summary

Source: without contents, identity
Phase 1: all contents
Phase 2: the contents important for the momentary situation
Phase 3: only one content

=> Here a development takes place from the consciousness itself about all contents, some contents to one content – thus an increasing orientation to the thing in the outside, which is momentarily most important.

II 1. e)   Abundance, strength and self-love

In the first three phases of development, three basic qualities emerge in the human being, which are then further developed in later life:

oral phase (0-1 year): abundance, security, basic trust = "Yes"
anal phase (1-3 years): strength, discrimination, clarity = "No!"
phallic phase (3-12 years): self-love = "Me!!!"

In the oral phase, one is one with everything (especially with the mother). There is no distinction between inside and outside – a comprehensive "Yes".
In the anal phase, a distinction is made between pleasant and unpleasant and the world is structured by this, creating rhythms – the toddler learns the word "No!".
In the phallic phase, the "I!!!" is finally found with the help of the "Yes" and the "No!".

Since this is an outward-inward development, the "Yes" of the oral phase corresponds to 'Phase 3' (root chakra and crown chakra), the "No!" of the anal phase corresponds to 'Phase 2' (hara and third eye), and the "Me!!!" of the phallic phase corresponds to 'Phase 1' (solar plexus and throat chakra).
This dynamic will be described in more detail later.

Summary

Phase 1: an unrestrained "yes" to oneself and a fierce "no" to all obstacles, i.e. an unrestrained "I!!!" → self-love

Phase 2: a discernment between "pleasant" (yes) and "unpleasant" (no), with the structuring "No!" being the new achievement → strength

Phase 3: an approving "yes" → fullness.

=> Here emerges increasing structuring and alignment.

II 1. f) Association, analogy and centering

The three phases just described have three different structuring principles:

- oral phase: association (similar things connect)
- anal phase: analogy (things with the same structure correspond)
- phallic phase: centering (everything is aligned to the center)

These three principles will be described in more detail later.

Summary

Phase 1: centering = "Me!!!"
Phase 2: analogy = "No!"
Phase 3: association = "Yes"

=> Here one can see an approach to the world.

II 1. g) Anticipation, joy and enjoyment

Three different basic feelings belong to the three phases:

> Phase 1: the anticipation of what one will create and experience is the impetus for doing anything at all.

> Phase 2: the joy of what is being created is, so to speak, the concretized anticipation.

> Phase 3: enjoying what one has achieved is the concretization of joy.

Summary

Phase 1: anticipation
Phase 2: joy
Phase 3: Enjoyment

=> Here an increasing concretization can be observed.

– History –

II 1. h) History

The first three phases of the psychic development of the individual human being are also found in the history of mankind. As in the development of the psyche, the historical phases have here the reverse order (this will be shown later in more detail).

> Phase 1: The people lived in the kingdom in a centrally controlled system, in which the king corresponds to the "I!!!" of the individual human being. The worldview was the philosophy in which all things are derived from a first cause (a correspondence to the "I!!!").

> Phase 2: The people lived in the Neolithic Age on the "islands of culture" in the "sea of nature". They shaped their environment by building villages, farming and raising livestock. This activity was symbolized by the grain god

("Yes"), whose brother and enemy had been the wilderness god ("No!"). The world view consisted of parables (analogies), which in their entirety formed the mythology.

Phase 3: Paleolithic people lived as part of nature in nature. They had a simple worldview based on associations with the mother ("Yes") at the center.

<u>Summary</u>

Phase 1: Kingship, centering
Phase 2: Neolithic, analogies
Phase 3: Paleolithic, associations

=> Here we find an increasing connection with the world.

– Economy –

II 1. i) The dynamics of an enterprise

Every company and to a limited extent every individual deed has three phases:

Source: First of all, there must be someone who wants to do something.

Phase 1: In this phase, the project is set in motion with all one's might, with full commitment, great enthusiasm and a lot of overtime.

Phase 2: In this phase, the project is structured, the processes are optimized and the behavior in it is defined by rules, and the working time is reduced to a level that is permanently feasible.

Phase 3: Finally, a flexibility must emerge that responds to each changing situation and thus finds a living rhythm that sometimes requires more, sometimes less work.

Summary

Phase 1: Foundation with a lot of momentum
Phase 2: Creation of a sustainable structure
Phase 3: Adaptation to the momentary situation

=> This process is the creation of a social organism.

– Everyday life –

II 1. j) Sending a letter

Even very simple processes like sending a letter show these three phases:

Phase 1: The letter must have enough strength – it must be sufficiently stamped.

Phase 2: The letter must have the right structure – it must be addressed correctly.

Phase 3: The letter must be grounded – it must be put into the mailbox.

Summary

Phase 1: sufficient postage
Phase 2: correct address
Phase 3: post the letter

=> This is a concretization process.

II 1. k) Composing a song

There are many ways to compose a song. The character of the resulting song depends on the way it is composed. The question is what is at the beginning:

> Source: an important theme (identity)
> Phase 1: a melody (feeling)
> Phase 2: a text (mind)
> Phase 3: an improvisation (experience)

If you first write a lyric and then find a melody to go with it, the song will tend to be head-oriented.

If one finds a melody first and then adds lyrics, the song will tend to be emotion-oriented (the way the Beatles composed most songs).

If one has the need to express something essential and then searches for a melody that corresponds to that essential by improvisation, and then adds appropriate words to that melody, the song will be very lively.

Of course, good songs can be created in any way – and there are also mixed forms, e.g. the possibility that at the beginning there was a text that expressed a basic feeling of the composer, who then found a melody and rewrote the text and adapted it to the melody.

Summary

Source: something essential
Phase 1: melody
Phase 2: lyrics
Phase 3: singing, improvosation

=> This is a concretization process, too.

II 1. l) Zodiac: cardinal, fixed and mutable

The twelve signs of the zodiac consist of three dynamics of each of the four elements. The elements are fire, water, air and earth; the three dynamics are cardinal, fixed and mutable. These three dynamics are another three-step.

Phase 1: cardinal = to found, to create, to start something

Phase 2: fixed = to structure something, to let it grow, to organize it

Phase 3: mutable = to respond to current circumstances

These 3 times four elements correspond to the four basic building blocks of the world, which come in four sizes:

The 12 Basic Elementary Particles and the Signs of the Zodiac			
	1st family *normal particles;* *cardinal zodiac signs*	*2nd family* *heavy particles;* *fixed zodiac signs*	*3rd family* *very heavy particles;* *mutable zodiacal signs*
quark 1 *fire*	„up"-quark *Aries*	„charm"-quark *Leo*	„truth"-quark *Sagittarius*
quark 2 *water*	„down"-quark *Cancer*	„strange"-quark *Scorpio*	„beauty"-quark *Pisces*
Leptons *Air*	Electron *Libra*	Muon *Aquarius*	Tauon *Gemini*
Neutrinos *Earth*	Electron neutrino *Capricorn*	Muon neutrino *Taurus*	Tauon neutrino *Virgo*

The exact analogy between the $3 \cdot 4 = 12$ signs of the zodiak and the also $3 \cdot 4 = 12$ elemantary particles is not known for sure – the analogy shown here is just a working hypothesis. The analogy of the three phases to the three dynamics (cardinal, fixed, mutable) is certain, but not the analogy of the four elements to the four kinds of particles.

Summary

Phase 1: cardinal
Phase 2: fixed
Phase 3: mobile

=> Here an increasing closeness to the world can be observed.

II 1. m)   Conjunction, opposition and trine

These three qualities also correspond to three astrological aspects, that is, three of the possible angles between the planets in a horoscope.

Phase 1: conjunction (0°) = unity, one direction, always together
=> a 0°-step stays at the initial place = "1".

Phase 2: Opposition (180°) = complementary opposites form structures
=> two 180°-steps lead back to the starting place = "2".

Phase 3: Trine (120°) = two planets are joined in cooperation
=> three 180°-steps lead back to the initial location = "3".

Summary

Phase 1: conjunction = unity ("1")
Phase 2: opposition = polarity ("2")
Phase 3: Trigon = commonality ("3")

=> These three steps describe the spanning of a space.

II 1. n) Consciousness, matter and the transition in between

The most basic three-step in magic is the inside of the world (consciousness), the outside of the world (matter) and the transition between the two (life force = magic).

Summary

Phase 1: Consciousness
Phase 2: Life force = magic
Phase 3: Matter

=> This is a creation process.

II 1. o) Concentration, analogy and enjoyment

In the subjective experience the three-step appears in magic as the unrestrained concentration on a goal, as the use of analogies and finally as the grounding or enjoying.

Summary

Phase 1: Concentration
Phase 2: Analogy
Phase 3: Grounding by savoring

=> This is a magical action.

II 1. p) Summary: the three phases

Now the results of the previous considerations can be combined to obtain in this way a sharp outline of the three phases.

Phase 1
In phase 1, everything is interconnected and has an unrestricted and uninhibited effect. Therefore, this state is unified and stable. In this state of consciousness, all contents are on an equal footing – everything is visible and everything has an effect. Everything is a part of the I, everything is filled with self-love and related to its origin in one's own soul in the heart chakra – a perfect expression of the soul. This area is completely inner-determined and completely independent of the outside. It is soul-centered. This state is creative, it is a wanting, a concentration, a pre-joy – the state of an omnipotent king in his domain. Here is found an unrestrained self-affirmation.

Phase 2
Phase 2 is less stable than Phase 1 because it is both inner-formed and outer-formed. Here the impulses coming from the soul (phase 1) are concretized on the basis of the possibilities in the world – which is why these concretizations can also change again and again. In this state contents are selected, which are taken up into the consciousness – those, which are of importance for the momentary situation. One accepts and rejects, one says "yes" and says "no". Here we find a differentiated evaluation of all things – and a corresponding action. Since it is about implementing what one chooses, "strength" is the central concept here – in addition to the clarity needed to recognize the situation. Situations are shaped and sustainable structures are created. One repeats pleasant things and proven strategies. By the success achieved in this way, joy is created. This creative designing also extends to making magic happen.

Phase 3

In Phase 3, everything is focused on a single point: the one-pointed presence in the here and now. This phase is the least stable or constant, as it always refers to the moment – this phase is characterized by a great mobility.

Here the consciousness has only one content and can therefore reach the state of ecstasy. One agrees with the situation and enjoys the moment. By this one is connected with what is there – one lives in abundance. One has contact with the world, one is associated with it, one experiences togetherness.

Thereby one co-shapes from the inside what is on the outside.

Development

The identity unfolds in three phases, which have different qualities. Thereby, the first phase of unrestrained self-love is always the foundation and the support – and phase 1 again rests in the identity, which simply is what it is.

The path from inside to outside begins with a perfect self-centeredness (phase 1) and develops by the meeting of inside and outside (phase 2) to a perfect presence in the world (phase 3). Therefore, phase 1 is always the same (as it relates to identity), while phase 2 gradually evolves according to getting to know the world and the possibilities it currently offers. Finally, phase 3 contains the experiencing of the world, i.e. a distinct world-relatedness and thus a constant change.

Phase 1 contains all contents of consciousness, phase 2 contains those which are relevant in the momentary situation and phase 3 contains only one content: the momentary experiencing. This can be understood as an increasing restriction of attention to a single thing in the outside. In the process, structure, orientation, concreteness, closeness to the world, and experiencing the outside increasingly emerge.

This process creates a space in which one moves, as well as social organisms in which one participates.

This is a process of creation, a magical action.

II 2.   The Bipolar Three-Step

The three-step described in the previous chapter as "phase 1/2/3" has in some cases two poles, i.e. it occurs twice. Here obviously the two-polarity of the electromagnetic force or the astrological opposition aspect has been combined with the three-step.

These two poles in the three-step are also found in some other systems and symbols which will be described below.

II 2. a)   The chakra system

The best-known two-pole three-step is the chakra system in which the three-step dynamic occurs both downward (solar plexus – hara – root chakra) and upward (throat chakra – third eye – crown chakra).

II 2. b)   The surrounding area of the sun

The second important bipolar three-step is the sun's surounding space, which is divided (as already shown) into the inner solar wind area (phase 1), the middle shock front area (phase 2) and the outer bow wave area (phase 3). The solar wind region is a spherical space around the Sun; the shock front and bow wave are spherical surface regions around the solar wind region.

The two electromagnetic jets (focused beams) reaching out into space from the north and south poles of the Sun traverse the three regions around the Sun in opposite directions. The two jets together with the three areas around the sun thus form two three-steps.

II 2. c)   The Vajra

This structure is also found in an Indo-Tibetan symbol: the Vajra. This symbol dates back to the middle Neolithic period in Mesopotamia.

The Vajra has a spherical center that expands symmetrically in opposite directions (sun, heart chakra).

The first expansion are the two lotus flowers (solar wind space, solar plexus/throat chakra).

The newly created form are the four elephant heads each emerging from the lotus (shock front, hara/third eye).

The contact is represented by the meeting of the four elephant trunks on the very outside (bow wave, root chakra/crown chakra). The two rods in the middle of each of the four elephant heads correspond to the two jets of the sun and to the sushumna.

Originally, the vajra was a symbol of lightning among the Indo-Europeans and the Neolithic peoples of Mesopotamia. It is also known from the magic wands of the Germanic seers, from the Greeks and Hittites and from the Sumerians and Babylonians.

- - -

From the analogy between the chakra system and the solar system two important conclusions arise:

- In the center of the sun's circumference is the sun, so in the center of the chakra system there must also be a "sun" – that is the soul.

The sun is the cause of the threefold structured environment of the sun (solar wind, shock front, bow wave) – without the sun this structure would not exist at all. Therefore, by analogy, there must be such a "sun" in the heart chakra – the soul.

61

- The solar system and also the chakra system are by their structure an expansion from a center, which leads in three steps to a concretization.

Since the chakra system is the basic structure of the psyche and thus of the consciousness of man, it follows from this dynamic of radiation, expansion and self-expression that this same urge to expand is also the basic dynamic of the soul.

II 2. d)   Summary: the bipolar three-step

The three-step appears twice in opposite directions in a system, if a bipolar force acts in this system.

Possibly this structure is more widespread than the two systems mentioned here and the one symbol suggest, since both the chakra system and the structure of the space, that surrounds the sun, are basic systems in the area of conscious and matter respectivly.

II 3.   The Extension to the Five-Step

In some of the examples of three-steps already discussed, the source of the three-step and also the outside, that is, the destination of the three-step, have already been mentioned. These two elements are always there in addition to the three-step and form thus the five-step.

II 3. a)   The chakras

The source of the three-step in the chakra system is the heart chakra. The identity in it is what expresses itself with the help of the three-step. This source is pure consciousness without a content.

The outside in the chakra system is the body and the whole material world. Matter is the outside of consciousness, just as consciousness is the inside of the material world.

At the point where consciousness and the material world touch, there is consciousness with contents of consciousness: this is the area of life force.

The consciousness, the transition area (life force) and the matter form the basic three-step in the world.

This "encounter-area" between consciousness and matter can be divided again into the three-step, which then results in a total of five steps:

The Emergence of the Five-Step		
1st step	*2nd step*	*3rd step*
world	consciousness	consciousness (without content)
	encounter area (consciousness with contents)	phase 1 (consciousness with all contents)
		phase 2 (consciousness with some content)
		phase 3 (consciousness with one content)
	matter	matter

II 3. b)   Deep sleep, subconsciousness, waking consciousness, ecstasy and matter

These five realms are found in man:

The Five Realms in a Human	
Consciousness	*Contents*
deep sleep consciousness (silence)	only consciousness without contents
subconsciousness	consciousness with all contents
waking consciousness	consciousness with some contents
ecstasy	consciousness with one content
body	only body without consciousness

The two poles are pure consciousness without contents and pure matter without consciousness.

II 3. c)   Energy, matter and "black hole substance"

The world consists fundamentally considered of four things: space-time, energy, matter and the "substance" of the black holes.

The basis of everything is the space-time – in it everything takes place. Both time and space are boundless. Space-time is the source of everything.

Space-time corresponds to the heart chakra, the deep sleep consciousness and the "house" in which the archive of the subconsciousness, the office of the waking consciousness and the desk lamp of the ecstasy state are located.

The first thing that was created in the world is energy. It spreads unhindered and endlessly in all directions with the speed of light – provided that it does not meet matter.

Energy corresponds to 'phase 1' which is characterized by the unrestrained and unrestricted self-expression.

This phase was extremely short: It lasted immediately after the big bang only 10^{-30} seconds. In this time the universe has expanded with the 10^{50}-fold speed of light ("inflationary universe").

The second thing which has originated in the world is the matter. It is limited ("solid") and moves slower than the speed of light ("c"). The relation between energy and matter is described by Einstein's famous formula "$E=mc^2$". This shows, when energy turns into matter, it becomes smaller by a factor of "c^2", i.e. it condenses, it encapsulates itself and loses the ability to move at the speed of light and acquires a solid boundary and thus a solid form.

Matter seems to correspond first of all to the 'phase 2' which is characterized by the emergence of solid forms, by demarcations, connections and opposites.

However, the 'time of matter', in which there were no black holes yet, consists of two very different sections, which differ by the behavior of the light:

In the first section, which has lasted after all 10,000 years after phase 1, the universe growing now only with light speed was still so small that the energy and the matter in it was so dense that the universe has been like a single gigantic sun.

Because of the high density and the high pressure in the universe at that time all things in it were equally distributed, equally far away from each other, equally hot, equally bright etc.. At that time the universe has had no centres like todays galaxies and suns. The state in which the protons, neutrons, electrons, neutrinos and energy quanta were at that time is called "thermal equilibrium".

In this first section the whole universe has been still one unit. It corresponds to the phase 2.

The second section began 10,000 years after the big bang. Now the universe was so big that differences in the density, in the heat and in the brightness could form: The "thermal disequilibrium" arose.

At the same time the first atoms with electron shell were formed, which is a process, which fits symbolically to the end of the thermal equilibrium, but is physically seen independent of it.

In this second section the whole universe is no more a unit, but consists of single independent units: Atoms, collections of atoms up to the formation of meteorites, moons, planets, suns and galaxies. This section corresponds to the phase 3.

The third thing that has been formed in the world (after energy and matter) are the black holes. They have been originally very big stars, which have been therefore also very heavy and have had a very great gravitation. These stars, which are in the center of galaxies, have attracted and "swallowed" more and more other stars, until they and their gravity have finally become so large that their entire mass has shrunk to a point and not even the light could fly away from them – which is why they appear as "black" when seen from the outside.

Also here, as in the condensation of the energy to matter, a condensation process takes place, in which matter is contracted to "black hole substance" ("x") in very small space (the whole matter of Earth would result in just $1 cm^3$ of black hole substance). Again, the speed of light ("c") is lost: light can no longer travel away from the black hole. Both processes have the same dynamics:

Energy => Matter: "$E=mc^2$".
Matter => black hole substance (x) "$m=xc^2$".

From this it follows that with the transformation of energy into "black hole substance" the transformation factor must be "c^4" ($c^2 \cdot c^2 = c^4$). This "c^4" is therefore also the central element in the formulas with which the properties of the black holes are described.

The "black hole substance" corresponds to the 'outside', the world, the "non-consciousness".

66

The big bang, in which space-time and afterwards from it energy originates, corresponds to the transition from the heart chakra to the solar plexus (wish-tree intermediate chakra) and to the throat chakra (thymus intermediate chakra).

The heart chakra itself corresponds to the "singularity", i.e. the state before the Big Bang, in which there was only one "something" that contained the entire world.

The two transitions between phase 1 and 2, between phase 2 and 3 as well as between phase 3 and outside take place only at a certain density:

Matter has formed only in the first 10,000 years after the big bang, when the energy density was still sufficiently great for it.

=> This process began at the beginning (big bang) and has therefore a temporal limit at its end.

The atoms have formed only after the density in the universe had become so small after 10,000 years that places of different density, heat and brightness could develop.

=> This process began after the first phase ended and continues until today in all stars in which heavy atoms are formed from light atoms. This process has begun immediately after the end of the thermal equilibrium as a general process everywhere in the then still nearly homogeneous universe and then, however, has become more and more isolated and takes place today only in the interior of the suns which have in their interior approximately the same state as the entire universe before the end of the thermal equilibrium.

The black holes can form only in the center of a galaxy where the density of matter is big enough.

=> This process can occur only if in the center of a galaxy a sufficient density of matter has been reached.

Summary

Source: singularity (unity) before the big bang

1st transition: inflationary universe (expansion with the 10^{50}-fold light speed)

Phase 1: energy expands unhindered with the speed of light.

2nd transition: formation of matter (quarks and electrons)

Phase 2: Matter is solid and moves slower than light. It is in a thermal equilibrium: The universe is everywhere equally dense, hot and bright. The whole unsiverse is, so to speak, one single, all-emcompassing sun.

3rd transition: End of thermal equilibrium and formation of atoms with electron shells.

Phase 3: Matter is solid and moves slower than light. It is no longer in thermal equilibrium: the universe is differentially dense, hot and bright, i.e. there are suns, planets, moons, light rays, different brightnesses, empty space, etc.

4th transition: At some places so much matter has accumulated that it collapses to almost a point and becomes a black hole.

Outside: the substance of a black hole is almost point-like and does not let light fly away from itself.

=> From 'phase 1' to 'phase 3' there are several developments:

   - The speed of motion decreases from the speed of light to a small speed to "0".
   - The solidity increases from "formless" to "formed" to "point-like".
   - Size shrinks from "vastness" to "boundedness" to "point".
   - Density of matter increases from "tiny" to "normal" to "almost endless".

The four transitions between the beginning (singularity), the three states, and the end (black hole) are condensation processes where pre-existing properties are encapsulated:

The first transition (singularity → phase 1) is the big bang: the unity before the diversity of the world (singularity) begins to differentiate and expand.

> *=> Transferred to the chakras, this means that the soul in the heart chakra (the "singularity" in the human being) creates a body out of itself and incarnates (the "human big bang", so to speak).*
>
> *The heart chakra radiates through the wish tree into the solar plexus and through the thymus intermediate chakra into the throat chakra.*

The second transition (phase 1 → phase 2) can only take place within the first 10,000 years after the big bang in the great energy density present there. So this state ends some time after its beginning.

> *=> Transferred to the chakras, this means that an impulse in the solar plexus only acts through the navel intermediate chakra into the hara if the intensity is sufficiently high, and also an impulse in the throat chakra only acts through the palate intermediate chakra into the third eye if the intensity is sufficiently high.*
>
> *Thus, the transformation of a general desire into a concrete desire occurs only when the intensity of the general desire is high enough.*

At the third transition (phase 2 → phase 3), a different distribution of light in the universe arises.

> *=> Transferred to the chakras, this means that there are alternating processes here, i.e. an alternation of event and rest, an alternation between different states and thus a rhythm.*
>
> *The impulses from the hara reach the root chakra through the pubic hair intermediate chakra only now and then, and likewise from the third eye through the main hair intermediate chakra to the crown chakra only now and then.*

The fourth transition (Phase 3 → Outside) can take place only when there is sufficient matter density in a galaxy center. This state must first be reached.

> *=> Transferred to the chakras, this means that the impulses in the root chakra and the crown chakra have an effect on the outside only if their intensity is great enough.*

> *The two intermediate chakras leading above and below from man to earth and heaven, respectively, are called "gate of earth" or "gate of fire" and "gate of heaven" or "gate of light," respectively.*

II 3. d)   Exercise of the Middle Pillar

The "Exercise of the Middle Pillar" is an important element of many meditations and rituals. It is a five-part pillar, that is, a pillar divided into "above", "above the middle", "middle", "below the middle" and "below".

It consists of five imaginations, which correspond to the five areas of the five-step. However, they are formulated in a more general way and related to the world as a whole:

the Middle Pillar				
Location	*Name*	*Area*	*Colour*	*God name*
top	Kether	God	white	Eheieh
above the center	Da'ath	deity	rainbow colours	Yod-Heh-Vau-He Elohim
centre	Tiphareth	soul	golden	Yod-Heh-Vau-He Eloha va-Da'ath
under the centre	Yesod	psyche	purple	Schaddai el-Chai
below	Malkuth	body	body	Adonai ha-Aretz

The "Middle Pillar Exercise" is performed as follows:

1. A few handbreadths above the head, Kether is imagined as a glistening white sphere, and at the same time God's name in Kether is intoned, i.e. sung on a constant tone as full-sounding as possible and ideally with over-tones and the natural vibrato of the voice: "Eheieh".

2. On the crown of the head, i.e. at the seat of the crown chakra, Da'ath is imagined as a sphere shining in the colors of the rainbow and the name of God in Da'ath is intoned: "Yod-He-Vau-He Elohim".

3. In the middle of the chest, at the seat of the heart chakra, Tiphareth is imagined as a golden yellow shining ball and the name of God in Tiphareth is

intoned: "Yod-He-Vau-He Eloha va-Daath".

4. Around the genitals, i.e. at the seat of the root chakra and thus of the kundalini snake, Yesod is imagined as a violet glowing sphere and God's name in Yesod is intoned: "Shaddai el-Chai".

5. Under the feet, i.e. in the earth, Malkuth is imagined as a brown sphere and the god's name of Malkuth is intoned: "Adonai ha-Aretz".

This exercise, as its structure shows, serves to intensify one's own radiance: the light of the center (Kether) is brought through a three-step (Da'ath, Tiphareth, Yesod) into the body (Malkuth).

II 4.   The Extension to the Eleven-Step

Just as one can extend the three-step to a five-step by differentiating the middle step, one can again divide the three middle steps into three steps each and thereby extend the five-step to an eleven-step. The origin and the result cannot be further divided into smaller units. So the differentiating sequence refers only to the transition between consciousness and matter, between inside and outside – and not to consciousness and matter itself.

From the Three-Step to the Eleven-Step		
Three-step	*Five step*	*Eleven step*
1 – 1 – 1	*1 – 3 – 1*	*1 – 9 – 1*
inside (source)	inside (source)	inside (source)
transition 1	transition 1	transition 1.1
		transition 1.2
		transition 1.3
	transition 2	transition 2.1
		transition 2.2
		transition 2.3
	transition 3	transition 3.1
		transition 3.2
		transition 3.3
outside	outside	outside

II 4. a)   The Kabbalistic Tree of Life

This division of the transition betwenn consciousness and matter ("life force") first into three steps and then the division of each of these three steps again into three substeps each has existed as a system for a long time and is represented as the Kabbalistic Tree of Life.

The inside (source, unity, God) is the topmost area on the Tree of Life; the outside (material world, body, human being) is the lowest area on the Tree of Life. The transition between these two consists of three successive areas, which in turn each consist of a triangle, each comprising three sub-areas (2/3/D, 4/5/6 and 7/8/9).

The Kabbalistic Tree of Life					
Differentiation			Sephiroth	Planet	Tree of Life
I	II	III			
1.	1.	1.	Kether	Pluto	
		2.	Chokmah	Neptun	
	2.	3.	Binah	Uranus	
		D	Da'ath	Saturn	
		4.	Chesed	Jupiter	
2.	3.	5.	Geburah	Mars	
		6.	Tiphareth	Sonne	
		7.	Netzach	Venus	
	4.	8.	Hod	Merkur	
		9.	Yesod	Mond	
3.	5.	10.	Malkuth	Erde	

On the Tree of Life there are four transitions corresponding to the intermediate chakras. They appear on the Tree of Life as horizontal lines, which have been drawn a little thinner in the graphic above to better distinguish them from the paths between the eleven areas.

These four transitions are:

- The "first cause" between 1 and 2/3/D: Here, seen from top to bottom, in the material world the energy quanta originate and in the area of consciousness the deities arise.

- The "abyss" between 2/3/D and 4/5/6: Here, seen from top to bottom, in the material world the elementary particles originate and in the area of consciousness the souls arise.

- The "trench" between 4/5/6 and 7/8/9: Here, seen from top to bottom, in the material world the atoms originate and in the area of consciousness the psyches come into being.

- The "threshold" between 9 and 10: Here, seen from top to bottom, in the material world the objects of everyday life arise and in the area of consciousness the bodies come into being.

II 4. b)   The superstring theory

The superstring theory used by physicists today is a very complex model. To describe it, a mathematical model is needed, which uses not only the three space dimensions and the one time dimension familiar from everyday life, but seven additional space dimensions, which, however, become visible only in areas far smaller than an electron. One of these seven additional dimensions has the property that it "envelops" the other ten dimensions, thus summarizes them and fits them together.

This eleven-dimensional mathematical model corresponds exactly to the Kabbalistic Tree of Life:

- The topmost of these eleven spheres (Kether) corresponds to the time dimension.

- The three spheres below it (Chokmah, Binah, Da'ath) correspond to the three "normal" space dimensions.

- The six following spheres (Chesed, Geburah, Tiphareth, Netzach, Hod, Yesod) correspond to the six "hidden" space dimensions.

- The lowest sphere (Malkuth) corresponds to the "summarizing" dimension.

The Tree of Life is the most differentiated analogy structure known so far. It consists of over 40 elements: the 11 spheres ("Sephiroth"), the 22 paths between them, the 3 triangles, the 4 transitions between the five areas on the Middle Pillar, etc.

The Kabbalistic Tree of Life is really literally found in everything from the structure of a cell and the evolution as a whole, to the German Constitution and the classical ballet, to a bee colony or a vacuum cleaner. This structure is found everywhere – even in the "heart of physics", as which one can call the superstring theory a little poetically.

A detailed description of this "inner structure of all things" may be found among others in my three books "Blossoms of the Tree of Life I -III".

II 5.   The Two Directions of the Three-Step

The Three-Step has been considered so far from the inside to the outside, but there is also the reverse direction.

II 5. a)   Unfolding and realization

Seen from the inside out, the Three Step is a creation, an action, an unfolding, a development, the evolution … In magic, this is telekinesis.

Seen from the outside inwardly, the three-step is a perception, a realization, an understanding, an involution, a rediscovery of the source … In magic, this is telepathy.

The ability to act in the realm of the life force (telekinesis) and the ability to perceive in the realm of the life force (telepathy) should be trained in approximately the same degree if one wants to become a magician or a sorceress, otherwise there could be difficulties. Doing something when you don't have an overview of the situation could be problematic – and likewise, having a perfect overview in combination with an inability to act is not very desirable either.

Unfolding and Cognition				
Area	*Unfolding*		*Cognition*	
inside	↓ identity		↑ cognition	
phase 1	↓	general desire (archetype)	↑	general description ("formula")
phase 2	↓	concrete wish (image)	↑	analysis (calculation)
phase 3	↓	experience, directing	↑	perception, contemplation
outside	↓ world		↑ object	

II 5. b) The "lightning ray of creation" and the "serpent of wisdom"

On the Kabbalistic Tree of Life, these two directions of movement have been represented by two symbols:

- The process of creation is represented by the "Lightning Ray of Creation," which is also called the "Sword of Creation." It follows the areas ("Sephiroth") from 1 to 10.

The cognition process is represented by the "Serpent of Wisdom", which is, among other things, also the rising Kundalini. It follows the 22 paths that connect the areas on the Tree of Life.

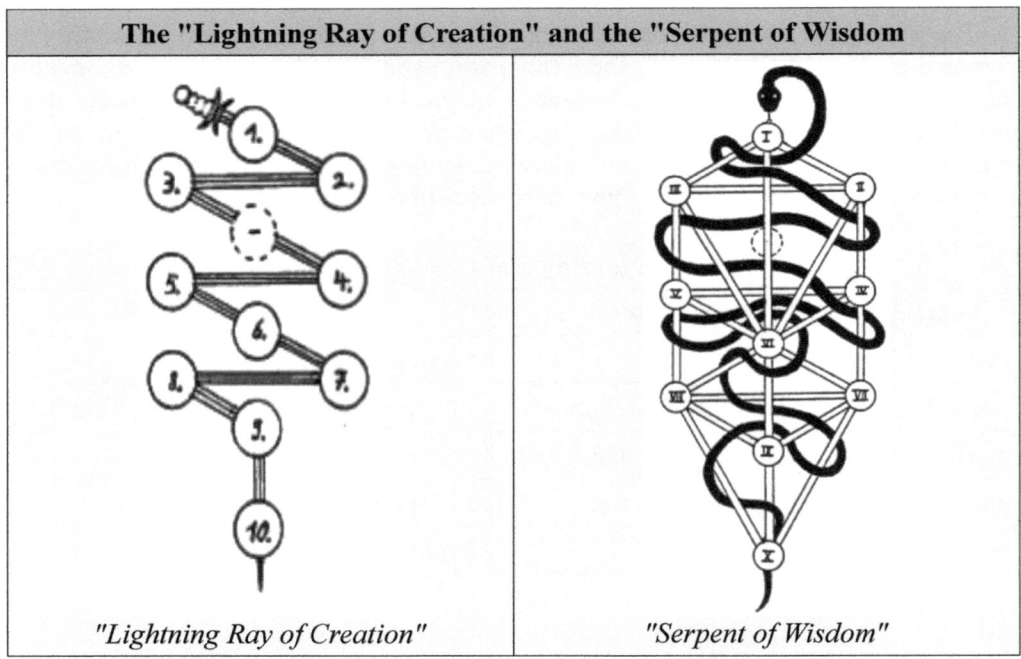

The "Lightning Ray of Creation" and the "Serpent of Wisdom

"Lightning Ray of Creation"   *"Serpent of Wisdom"*

II 5. c) Tummo and Bindhu

In India and in Tibet, these two directions of the three-step are distinguished in Yoga:

The process of creation is described as white light flowing down from above. It is called "Bindhu". In the Upanishads this process is described quite poetically as the "milking of the sky cow" – the blessing of the mother goddess is called down, which is understood as her milk. This is among other things also the origin of the ritual potion symbolism, which in India and in Europe finally led to the motive of the elixir of life.

The process of understanding is in India and Tibet firmly connected with the rising of the Kundalini. It is her heat, as a rule, which is the cause of the light of the celestial cow flowing down into the yogi.

II 5. d) Serpent and eagle

In some myths, the celestial light appears as an eagle and the earth fire appears as a serpent. Mythologically, these are the two images for the astral body, that is, for the souls of the living and the dead.

The soul-bird is the soul, which one can experience at a near-death as an astral body, i.e. as a leaving of the physical body, whereupon one can float freely around – one flies like a bird …

The snake is the dead man in his grave in the earth, where also the snakes live in caves, rock crevices and the like.

II 5. e) Big bang and $E=mc^2$

In physics the creation process is found as big bang and the cognition process as the condensation of energy to matter and as the condensation of matter to black holes.

II 5. f) Birth and death

The two most archaic images for the creation are procreation and birth and for the cognition process the afterlife journey and death.

II 6.   The Pulsating Three-Step

The presence of two directions of movement in the three-step already suggests that there is not only a simultaneity of these two directions (creation and cognition), but also a rhythmic alternation between both.

II 6. a)   Waking and sleeping

The most vivid example of such a rhythmic alternation is "playing one's instrument" while awake during the day and "tuning one's instrument" while asleep at night.

The day is mainly filled with self-expression and only to a small extent with cognition – e.g. during reflection, therapy or meditation.

At night, the experiences are first inserted into the subconscious mind during the dream phases and then thea are also tuned into the soul during the deep sleep phases.

This cycle keeps the whole human system intact.

II 6. b)   The development of the psyche

This rhythm also exists in life on a large scale. A total of four stages of life can be distinguished.

For a simpler overview, the sections that run from phase 1 to phase 3 (creation process) are written in normal letters, while the sections that run from phase 3 to phase 1 are written in italics.

Section 1:   Pregnancy
1.1 Subsection (Origin):
conception to end of the 6th month: only the EEG waves of deep sleep are detectable.
1.2 Subsection (Phase 1):
7 and 8 months: The EEG waves of subconsciousness are also detectable.
1.3 Subsection (phase 2):
9 month: EEG waves of waking consciousness are also detectable.

78

2nd phase: Childhood

2.1 Subsection (phase 3):

oral phase (the first year of life): the child lives in a unity with its mother and absorbs all impressions. Ideally, it experiences security and fullness in this phase and can develop the basic trust. This is a comprehensive "Yes".

2.2 Subsection (Phase 2):

anal phase (the second and third years of life): The child learns to walk, to talk and to say "No!". He learns to discriminate, to delimit, to take a stand and to choose. In this phase, the child develops his strength.

2.3 Substage (Phase 1):

phallic phase (approx. 3-12 years): the child learns to say "I!!!" on the basis of the "Yes" and the "No!" that it has already learned. This is the stage where self-love emerges.

Section 3:   Adolescence and adulthood.

- Connection:

This section connects to phase 1 ("I!!!") of the previous section and therefore begins with a phase 2.

3.1 Subsection (Phase 2):

genital phase (approx. 12-21 years): The adolescent turns to the world with his ego and searches for possibilities of expression and experience: Which relationship partner? Which profession? Which place of residence? During puberty, the adolescent tests his or her strength in the world. This phase is a "You?"

3.2 sub-phase (phase 3):

The adult phase (approx. 20-45 years): The adult has founded a family and created a space of security himself, in which he now lives. The "I!!!" and the "You?" have become a "We."

Section 4: Age

- Connection:

This section connects to phase 3 ("We.") of the previous section and therefore begins with a phase 2.

4.1 Subsection (Phase 2):

tutorial phase (about 45-70 years): the older adult, when the children have grown up, turns back to the world, develops *new hobbies, undertakes travel and begins to teach others. This phase is an "Other ..."*

4.2 Subsection (Phase 1):

gerontal phase (about 70 years to death): the old person reflects on the essentials and becomes wise. The "We." and the "Other ..." have become an "All".

5th stage: in the hereafter

The soul is now no longer incarnated and is in the beyond until a new incarnation.

The dynamics of these five phases of life become clearer if they are represented in a graph:

The Biographical Development					
Section	*Phase*				
	Soul in the heart chakra	*Phase 1* *throat chakra solar plexus*	*Phase 2* *third eye hara*	*Phase 3* *crown chakra root chakra*	*World*
before conception	soul				
1-6 month	deep sleep				
7-8 month		subconscious			
9 month			waking		
oral phase				*baby*	
anal phase			toddler		
phallic phase		child			
genital phase			adolescent		
adult phase				adult	
tutorial phase			*elder*		
gerontal phase		*old man*			
after death	soul				

80

A detailed description of this dynamic and also its analogy in history can be found in my book "Die sieben Schritte des Lebens".

II 6. c)   The development of mankind

The same structure and dynamics as in biography are also found in the history of mankind.

1. <u>Oral phase and Paleolithic period</u>: Both are characterized by a symbiosis with the environment: a "Yes".
Paleolithic people lived in nature as part of nature. The archetype was the Great Mother.

2. <u>Anal phase and Neolithic period</u>: Both are characterized by the importance of demarcation and shaping the environment while maintaining insertion into the rhythm of the environment: a "No!"
Neolithic people created islands of culture in nature: they practiced agriculture and animal husbandry and built villages and temples. The archetype for culture was the grain god, the archetype for nature was the wilderness god.

3. <u>phallic phase and kingship</u>: Both are a central control of the whole, the subordination of the system to a center, the shaping of the whole by a single will: an "I!!!"
The people in kingship "subdued the earth". The archetype was the One God.

4. <u>Genital phase and materialism</u>: Both are a researching and using, a knowing and enjoying, an exploring and shaping, a meeting and examining and choosing: a "You?"
Humans have achieved a previously unknown prosperity and a completely new extent of imprinting the earth's surface by the industrial revolution – the earth has become the "planet of the humans".

5. <u>Adult phase and globalization</u>: Both create a firm connection, a stable system, a sustainable basis: a "We".
The task of the people is now to find a collective way of life by which they do not destroy themselves.

6. <u>Tutorial phase and future I</u>: Both widen the possibility, seek new variants,

new encounters, learn and teach, give and receive: an "Other ..."

7. <u>Gerontal phase and future II</u>: Both seek unity, essence, wisdom, freedom: the "All".

History and Biography		
History	*Biography*	*Phases*
big bang	procreation	-
prehistory	pregnancy 1-6 month	(deep sleep /soul)
	pregnancy 7-8 month	1
	pregnancy 9 month	2
paleolithic	oral phase	3
neolithic	anal phase	2
kingship	phallic phase	1
materialism	genital phase	2
globalization	adult phase	3
future I	tutorial phase	2
future II	gerontal phase	1

II 6. d) Association, analogy and centering

The three phases each have a certain way of looking, which is also shown in the sections of human history. These three ways of looking and thinking are:

- <u>Phase 1</u>: association
- <u>Phase 2</u>: analogy
- <u>Phase 3</u>: centering

These three principles of order are applied to ever new life circumstances in the individual stages:

Baby – oral phase / Paleolithic: Associations

The baby first forms its world view by associations: people, beings and things acquire a certain quality by the memories of experiences with them.

The same is true for the worldview of the Paleolithic with the mother in the center.

The "Yes" of this epoch stands in a comprehensive network of associations (phase 1).

Toddler – anal phase / Neolithic: Analogies

The toddler forms its world view by dividing into "pleasant" and "unpleasant" and by the experience of being able to shape the environment by its own power. In the process, certain general categories are developed, which, together with rhythmic repetition, result in a worldview of analogies: for example, there is the same "putting to bed" ritual every night.

The same applies to the world view of the Neolithic with its myths, which are the description of such analogies.

The "No!" of this epoch stands in a systematic structure of analogies (phase 2).

Child – phallic phase / Kingship: Centering

The child forms its world view by recognizing itself as the center of its own world - it begins to want.

The same is true for the worldview of kingship with its centering, its monotheism and its philosophy.

The "I!!!" of this epoch stands in the middle of a mandala, which is created by a general centering (phase 3).

Adolescent – genital phase / Materialism: Analogies

The adolescent forms his world view by exploring the world whose structures he tries to fathom – including the structures and rhythms within himself.

The same is true of the worldview of materialism, which examines the world and describes it by "scientific analogies," that is, by formulas and diagrams.

The "You?" of this epoch stands in a systematic structure of analogies (phase 2).

Adult – adult phase / Globalisation: Association

The <u>adult</u> forms his worldview by including the people important to him into a family in which everyone is connected to everyone else.

The same applies to the world view of globalization, since the mutual dependence of all on each other is the basis and on it a stable system is built.

The "We." of this epoch stands in a comprehensive network of associations (phase 1).

Older Person – tutorial phase / Future I: Analogies

The <u>older person</u> forms his world view by his newly acquired freedom, leisure time and possibilities. He passes on his knowledge, formulates it in a generally valid way and explores new areas of life.

The same is likely to be true of the worldview of <u>Future I</u>, in which different ways of living are likely to be explored. These "life-designs" are a collection of possibilities, of biography-myths – of possible analogies to models.

The "Other ..." of this epoch stands in a systematic structure of analogies (phase 2).

Old Person – gerontal phase / Future II: Centering

The <u>old person</u> forms his world view by looking at the whole, as the part of which he experiences himself.

The same applies presumably also to the world picture <u>Future II</u>, in which humans will experience themselves presumably as a single "human being".

The "all" of this epoch stands in the middle of a mandala, which is created by a general centering (phase 3).

II 7. The Expansion to the Collective Three-Step

The development in the three-step of the individual human being is related to the corresponding processes in humanity and in the world as a whole.

II 7. a) Inside: source

The source is consciousness, which in its essence is a unity.

II 7. b) Phase 1: archetypes

Phase 1 corresponds to the subconscious in an individual. This individual phase is part of the collective subconscious. The images in the individual subconscious are connected to the archetypes (deities, myths) in the collective subconscious.

In this phase the connection is comprehensive: all images of the individual subconsciousness are also part of the collective subconscious.

II 7. c) Phase 2: politics

Phase 2 corresponds to the waking consciousness in an individual. This individual phase is part of the collective waking consciousness. The decisions and actions of the individual are part of the decisions and actions of humanity and thus part of politics.

In this phase, the connections are part of an overall structure, but not effective in everything: Many individual decisions and actions also influence the decisions and actions of other people.

II 7. d) Phase 3: collective experience

Phase 3 corresponds to experiencing in an individual person. This individual phase is part of the collective experience. The experience of the individual is often connected with the experience of one or more other people.

In this phase, a connection occurs only occasionally: Some things are experienced together with another person.

II 7. e) Outside: matter

Matter in the outside is a multiplicity in which each atom stands for itself.

II 7. f) Overview

The degree of connection decreases from the inside to the outside. This corresponds to the increasing concreteness from the inside to the outside.

The Degree of Connectedness		
individual	*collective*	*connectedness*
deep sleep consciousness	comprehensive consciousness (God)	unity
subconsciousness	collective subconsciousness	general connectedness
waking consciousness	politics	general influence
ecstasy consciousness	encounter	occasional encounter
body	material world	separated multiplicity

II 8. The Three-Step as Part of the Twelve-Divided Circle

The three-step does not stand isolated in the world, but is part of a more comprehensive system.

II 8. a)   The elementary particles

The three-step is found as the three quantities of the four basic elementary particles. The overview of these $3 \cdot 4 = 12$ elementary particles has already been given.

The 12 fundamental elementary particles

the 12 basic elementary particles			
	1st family normal particles (phase 1)	2nd family heavy particles (phase 2)	3rd family very heavy particles (phase 3)
quark 1	"up"-quark	„charm"-quark	„truth"-quark
quark 2	„down"- quark	„strange"- quark	„beauty"- quark
leptons	electron	muon	tauon
neutrinos	electron neutrino	muon neutrino	tauon neutrino

II 8. b)   The zodiac

Also the zodiac consists of $4 \cdot 3 = 12$ signs: 4 elements $\cdot$ 3 dynamics. As already described, the 12 signs of the zodiac correspond to the 12 basic elementary particles.

The 12 Basic Elementary Particles and the Signs of the Zodiac			
	1st family *normal particles;* *cardinal zodiac signs*	*2nd family* *heavy particles;* *fixed zodiac signs*	*3rd family* *very heavy particles;* *mutable zodiacal signs*
quark 1 *fire*	„up"-quark *Aries*	„charm"-quark *Leo*	„truth"-quark *Sagittarius*
quark 2 *water*	„down"-quark *Cancer*	„strange"-quark *Scorpio*	„beauty"-quark *Pisces*
Leptons *Air*	Electron *Libra*	Muon *Aquarius*	Tauon *Gemini*
Neutrinos *Earth*	Electron neutrino *Capricorn*	Muon neutrino *Taurus*	Tauon neutrino *Virgo*

II 8. c)   The superstring

The superstring is the blueprint of all elementary particles and all energy quanta, thus of all substance in our world. A superstring is like a circular string vibrating as a standing wave. The simplest superstring has exactly twelve waves of the same size and thus the same structure as the zodiac.

The standing wave is one of the very few physical phenomena that consists of a group of equally sized and sharply defined areas – and is thus an equivalent to the zodiac with its twelve equally sized and sharply defined zodiac signs.

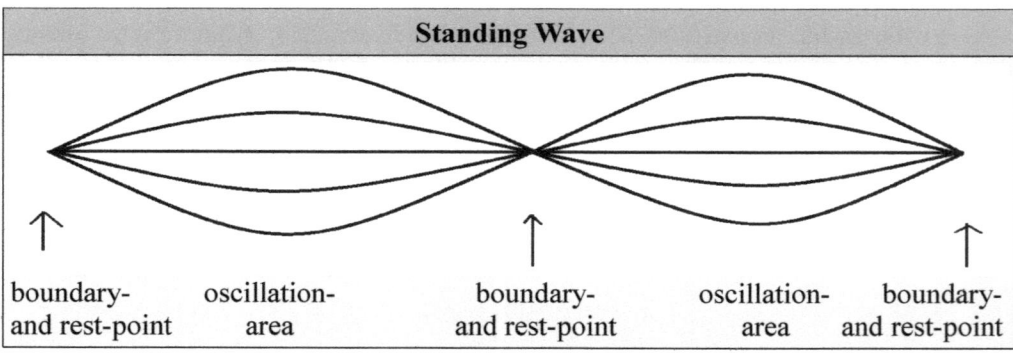

Standing Wave

| boundary-
 and rest-point | oscillation-
 area | boundary-
 and rest-point | oscillation-
 area | boundary-
 and rest-point |

Both the zodiac and Heisenberg spin chains (superstring) have the structure of a twelve-part circular standing wave:

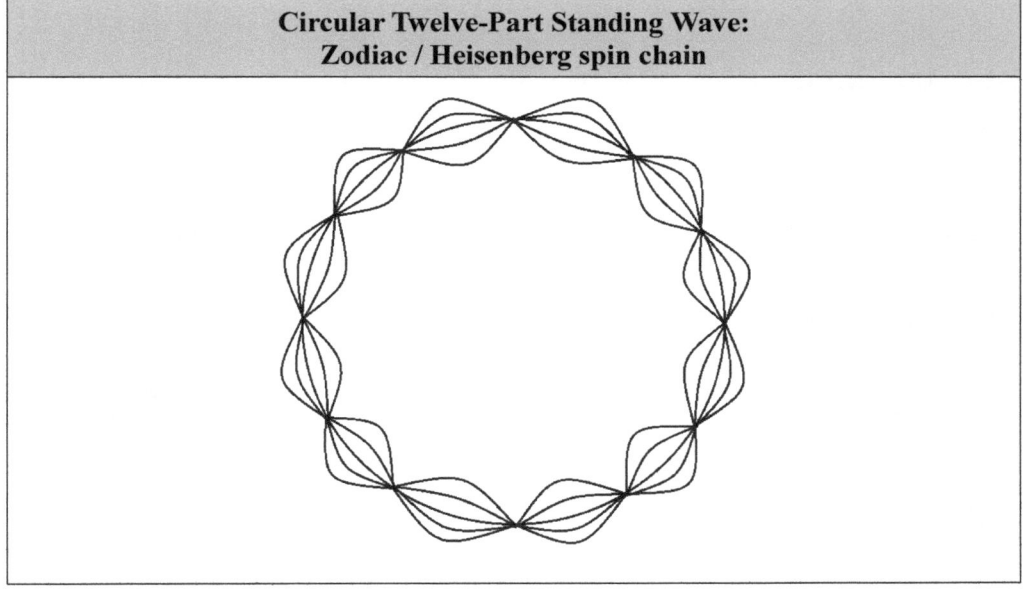

**Circular Twelve-Part Standing Wave:
Zodiac / Heisenberg spin chain**

Each wave crest corresponds to a zodiac sign. The unmoved zero points of this standing wave are the boundaries between the zodiacal signs.

II 8. d)   The zodiac on the Tree of Life

The transitions on the Kabbalistic Tree of Life each have the twelve-part structure of the zodiac.

Here again is the Tree of Life diagram with the four transitions (four thin horizontal lines):

The Kabbalistic Tree of Life					
Differentiation			**Sephiroth**	**Planet**	**Tree of Life**
I	*II*	*III*			
1.	1.	1.	Kether	Pluto	
		2.	Chokmah	Neptune	
	2.	3.	Binah	Uranus	
		D	Da'ath	Saturn	
		4.	Chesed	Jupiter	
2.	3.	5.	Geburah	Mars	
		6.	Tiphareth	Sun	
		7.	Netzach	Venus	
	4.	8.	Hod	Merkury	
		9.	Yesod	Moon	
3.	5.	10.	Malkuth	Earth	

These four transitions have the following character:

- the "first cause" between 1 and 2/3/D: Here, seen from top to bottom, the energy quanta arise in the material world and the deities in the consciousness realm originate.

The twelve-part structure is found here as the 12-part superstring.

- the "abyss" between 2/3/D and 4/5/6: Here, seen from top to bottom, the elementary particles develop in the material world and the souls in the area of consciousness.

The twelve-part structure is found here as the 12 basic elementary particles and as the zodiac around a planet or similar.

- the "trench" between 4/5/6 and 7/8/9: Here, seen from top to bottom, in the material world the atoms arise and in the consciousness area the psyches originate.

The twelve-part structure is found here as the forms of the electron shell of an atom and as a birth chart.

- the "threshold" between 7/8/9 and 10: Here, seen from top to bottom, in the material world the objects arise and in the consciousness realm the bodies originate.

The twelve-part structure is found here as the astrological transits.

II 8. e)   The three phases and the zodiac

The twelve-part structure is obviously a structure of transitions. Since the five areas between which these four "astrological" transitions are found, are the inside, the three phases and the outside, this twelve-part structure is also related to the intermediate chakras.

These twelve-part structures look a little different from the twelve-part structures on the Tree of Life, because here we are looking at the chakras of a person and thus his different resolutions and actions.

The Twelve-Part Structure and the Phases		
Areas	*Chakras*	*twelve-part structure*
inside	heart chakra	
intermediate chakra	*thymus intermediate chakra* *wish-tree intermediate chakra*	*birth chart* *of a human being*
phase 1	throat chakra solar plexus	
intermediate chakra	*palatal intermediate chakra* *navel intermediate chakra*	*horoscope of a* *general impulse*
phase 2	third eye hara	
intermediate chakra	*main hair intermediate chakra* *pubic hair intermediate chakra*	*horoscope of a* *concrete impulse*
phase 3	crown chakra root chakra	
intermediate chakra	*gate to heaven* *gate to the earth*	*horoscope of a moment* *(astrological transits)*
outside	body	

The transitions from one phase to the next are the places and times where a horoscope is created.

Obviously, the resolutions at the intermediate chakras, that is, at the transitions from one chakra to the next, are also such processes of creation by which a hroscope, that is, a twelve-part zodiacal imprint, is formed. At these transitions a determination, a reduction of the possibilities, a concretization and a shaping takes place – thus an astrological imprinting. This astrological imprinting can be calculated and checked for every decision.

II 8. f) Aspects and angles

The zodiac is a fixed system of twelve qualities. These twelve properties, i.e. the signs of the zodiac, are in certain relationships to each other. Each sign of the zodiac is a twelfth of a circle, i.e. 30° in size. Therefore, the relationships of the zodiac signs to each other can be described in 30° units – these are the astrological aspects.

conjunction (0°): the inseparable commonality of two planets, a "marriage", the identity, the unipolar gravitation

opposition (180°): the complementary opposition, the swing, the rhythm, the cycle, the change, yin and yang, movement, the bipolar electromagnetic force, the two poles of the bipolar triad (solar system, chakra system, vajra)

trine (120°): a friendship, the commonality of different items, a solid connection, commitment, the three-polar color force, the three-step

square (90°): a separation, a right angle, a tent pole, space, freedom, mutual acceptance of difference and joy in it, the four elements, the right angle between the electric wave and the magnetic wave

sextile (60°): the gathering of similars into a group, the "little trine", several moons in the same orbit, snowflakes, honeycombs, arrangement of spheres of the same size, "flower of life"

semi-sextile (30°): developmental step, moving on, transformation, metamorphosis, growth

quincunx (150°): integration, change, care, tension-building, ordering, healing, repairing

The zodiac obviously contains within itself these seven qualities. By them a new form is built up, which arises at a transition – both an astrological imprint and a new physical state (space-time $\rightarrow$ energy $\rightarrow$ matter in thermal equilibrium $\rightarrow$ matter in thermal disequilibrium $\rightarrow$ black hole).

Interestingly, the speed of light ("c") is closely coupled to these transitions, as the considerations in an earlier chapter have shown.

1st transition ("first cause"): At the big bang light, i.e. energy quanta (c) is created.

2nd transition ("abyss"): At the transformation of energy into matter a c^2 is lost ($E=mc^2$).

3rd transition ("trench"): At the end of the thermal equilibrium the uniform distribution of light (energy) and also of matter in the universe ends and light and shadow are created.

4th transition ("threshold"): At the formation of a black hole again a c^2 is lost (m = "black hole substance" · c^2).

What does this connection mean?

Light is the first that has come into being after the space-time and the gravity which is a property of the space-time … "Let there be light!". Light represents therefore the creation impulse and the maximum freedom which has been perfect in the first 10^{-30} seconds after the big bang.

The emergence of light at the transition 1 can be interpreted as creation impulse: A free space is created, which is filled by light.

The loss of the light at the transitions 2, 3 and 4 are concretizations: the choice of a possibility is always connected with a reduction of the freedom, because one has chosen one of many possibilities. At the end the freedom has arrived at "0", because one experiences something quite concrete in the here and now – this corresponds to the matter shrunk to a point in a black hole.

The black hole is "black" … no more light … and it is almost point-shaped … no more freedom … but maximum intensity and uniqueness …

II 8. g)   The quality of the numbers 1, 2, 3, 4, 5, 6 and 12

From the considerations about the zodiac it follows that some numbers have a natural symbolism.

The number **1** is the identity: the astrological conjunction (0° angle) and the gravitation.

The number **2** is the complementary opposition: the astrological opposition (180° angle) and the electromagnetic force.

The number **3** is the organic connection: the astrological trine (120° angle; three trines form a triangle), the color force and the three-step.

The number **4** is the separation, the vastness, the space and the freedom: the astrological square (90° angle; four square aspects form a geometrical square), the angle between electric wave and magnetic wave.

The number **5** is the integration and the healing: the astrological quincunx (150°).

The number **6** is the grouping: the astrological sextile (60°; six sextiles form a honeycomb).

The number **12** is the development and the complete: the astrological semi-sextile (30°; twelve semi-sextiles form a dodecagon) and also the zodiac itself.

One can use these numbers, since they have a fixed symbolism, also in the magic – e.g. as a symbol, with imaginations or with the production of talismans. This number symbolism looks briefly as follows:

Phase 1:   Solar plexus and throat chakra.

The **1** helps to center and achieve uniqueness and single-mindedness: the function of phase 1.

The **5** helps to order, heal and restore tension: an auxiliary function of phase 1.

94

Phase 2: Hara and Third Eye

The **2** helps to distinguish and find a suitable rhythm: the function of phase 2.

The **4** helps to delineate and create a clear form: an auxiliary function of phase 2.

Phase 3: Root chakra and crown chakra

The **3** helps to express oneself and create an organic form: the function of phase 3.

The **6** helps to find like-minded people and allies and to form a group: an auxiliary function of phase 3.

The intermediate chakras

The **12** helps to take the next step and stay in the flow: it helps to keep the movement between the three phases intact.

A detailed description of the symbolism of numbers may be found in my book "Number Symbolism for Beginners".

II 8. h) The Vajra

The vajra, also called the "thunderbolt" because it was originally a lightning symbol, also contains a twelve-part structure.

The Vajra

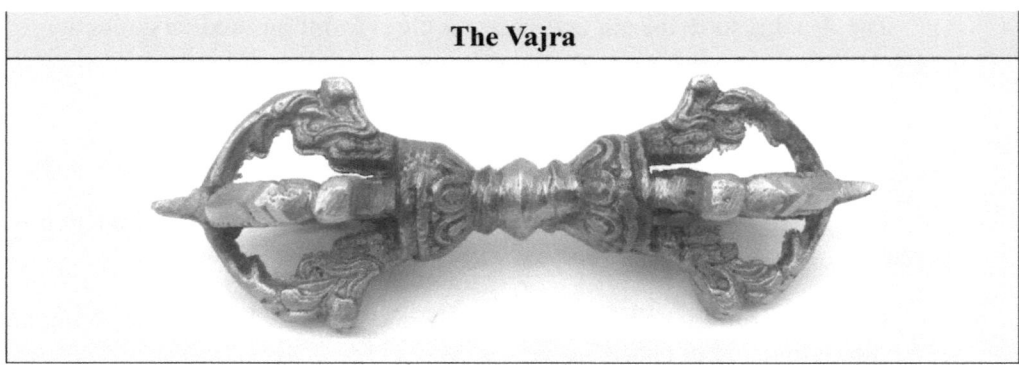

The sphere or discus in the middle is the center and the origin: God, the soul, and the like.

The symmetrical structure of the vajra corresponds to the "2", that is, the opposition, the yin/yang opposition, etc., which is also found in the chakra system (upper and lower chakras) and in the solar system (the jet at the north pole and the jet at the south pole).

The two lotus flowers are the unimpeded unfoldment of phase 1.

The twice four elephant heads are the formation of a phase 2 structure.

The two times four elephant trunks are the experiencing in the here and now of phase 3.

The four number of elephants corresponds to the four elements in the zodiac and the three number of phases (lotus, elephant head, elephant trunk) corresponds to the three forms in which each element occurs in the zodiac. Thus, the symbolism of the twelve (3·4=12) is also found here – but it's no important symbolism in the vajra.

The two rays in the center correspond to the quintessence, which can be understood as the guidance of the four elements in the three phases by the origin (centre, heart chakra, soul).

II 9.   The Transitions Between the Three Phases

The transitions between the three phases correspond to the four intermediate chakra pairs and the four transitions on the Kabbalistic Tree of Life.

They are the "gates of unfoldment" and thus "lightning ray of creation" in the Tree of Life:

> New forms are created at these transitions,
> they are the places of transformation,
> they are the places of decision,
> they are the gates of concretization,
> at them the astrological imprint is born,
> at them freedom is exchanged for decision,
> at them light becomes delimitation,
> here creative magic is born,
> here is born telekinesis,
> here self-expression is born,
> they are the path to experiencing the world,
> they are the path to matter,
> they are the avenue to the outside...

They are also the "gates of knowledge" and thus the "snake of wisdom" in the Tree of Life:

> At these crossings, new knowledge emerges,
> they are the places of encounter with trauma,
> they are the places of healing,
> they are the gates of return,
> at them the astrological imprint is dissolved,
> at them are the places where decision is exchanged for freedom,
> at them are the places where separation becomes light,
> here discerning magic is born,
> here telepathy arises,
> here self-knowledge arises,
> they are the path of return to one's own soul,
> they are the path to consciousness,
> they are the avenue to the inside...

The intermediate chakras are obviously the places in the chakra system that are most important for magic as well.

II 10. The Disturbances of the Three-Step

As in all complex systems, disturbances can occur in the chakra system, the healing of which is of great importance for the well-being of the person concerned.

II 10. a) The chakra polarizations

Disturbances in the flow of the soul's impulses from the inside to the outside lead to the already described polarizations of the three qualities "self-love", "strength" and "abundance" which correspond to the three phases.

In these disturbances there is a life force congestion in one of the six outer chakras and parallel to this in each case a life force deficiency in the other chakra of the chakra pair concerned.

Instead of "life force congestion in one chakra" one can also say "fixation on one chakra" and instead of "life force deficiency in one chakra" one can also say "avoidance of one chakra".

These extreme states already described are:

- life force congestion in the solar plexus: egocentric star
- life force congestion in the throat chakra: shameful fan

- life force congestion in the hara: ruthless perpetrator
- life force congestion in the third eye: fearful victim

- life force congestion in the root chakra: deliquescent addict
- life force congestion in the crown chakra: hardened ascetic

II 10. b) The blockages at the transitions

If there is a life force congestion, there must be a blockage, a dam, a closed gate... This can only be an intermediate chakra in the case of the congestion of a chakra.

Since the impulses flow outward from the heart chakra, the blockage that jams the life force in a chakra must be on the outside of that chakra, that is, on the side away from the heart chakra.

On the other hand, for the chakra with the life force deficiency, the blockage should be on the side facing the heart chakra, since no life force can reach this chakra from it.

This results in the following six possible constellations of disturbances in the chakras.

These disturbances of the psychic structure and therefore of the well-being of the person concerned also affect the practice of magic, since the life force cannot flow freely from the heart chakra to the outside and thus be creative.

For every kind of disturbance there is, of course, also a specific way of healing.

Phase 1:   Disturbances in the inner pair of chakras

1. The **star** with delusions of grandeur:

> 1.1 The life force congestion in the solar plexus arises from a blockage in the umbilical intermediate chakra:
>> - The star is unable to move out of its ego-centeredness (life force congestion in the solar plexus) into world-centeredness (hara) – the life force remains trapped and isolated in its delusions of grandeur.
>> - The magic of the star remains stuck in self-praise.

> 1.2 The lack of vitality in the throat chakra arises from a blockage in the thymus intermediate chakra:
>> - The star is afraid to direct his attention to others (activity of the throat chakra), to listen to them and to take them as important, because he fears that he will then come to receive too little attention himself – so he closes his thymus minor chakra and looks only at himself.
>> - The star is not able to cooperate with others in magic, but always sees others only as fame competitors.

>> => The star becomes a pompous "show magician" ...

>> => Healing: The star may expand himself more and more until he finally experiences himself as God – and thus finds again the source of life in the Unio mystica ... the egocentric will-magician.

2. The **fan** with the inferiority complex:

2.1 The life force congestion in the throat chakra is caused by a blockage in the palate intermediate chakra:

- The fan is not able to go from his you-centeredness (life force congestion in the throat chakra) into concrete resolutions in community life that are associated with a willingness to conflict (third eye) – he remains trapped and isolated in his inferiority complex.

- The magic of the fan remains stuck in the imitation of his ideal.

2.2 The lack of life force in the solar plexus arises from a blockage in the wish tree intermediate chakra:

- The fan is afraid to show himself (activity of the solar plexus) because he fears being ridiculed and then being ashamed. Therefore, he refrains from letting his identity (heart chakra) become general wishes (solar plexus) – so he closes his wish-tree intermediate chakra and does not dare to show himself (solar plexus activity).

- In magic, the fan is not able to care about the fulfillment of his own needs – he always looks only at the needs of others.

=> The fan becomes a master-worshipping "follower-magician" …

=> Healing: The fan may devote himself to a deity in loving worship – and by this Bhakti-Yoga return to himself ... the God-longing mystic.

3. The **perpetrator** in the attack posture:

3.1 The life force congestion in the hara arises from a blockage in the pubic intermediate chakra:

- The perpetrator is not able to move out of his aggressive attack posture (life force congestion in the hara) into the concrete experience and intimate physical encounter (root chakra) – he remains trapped and isolated in his aggression.

- The magic of the perpetrator remains stuck in the fight against supposed enemies.

3.2 The lack of vitality in the third eye is caused by a blockage in the palatal intermediate chakra:

- The perpetrator is afraid to look more closely at other people (activity of the third eye) because he fears that he will then fall short himself and be taken advantage of. Therefore, he closes his eyes to the sight of others – he blocks his palatal intermediate chakra and does not dare to relax and look outward or even trust another person (third eye activity).

- In magic, the perpetrator is unable to stop his constant struggle and let go of his feeling of being threatened, which causes him to live separate from everyone else and from the world.

=> The perpetrator becomes a lonely "power magician" …

=> Healing: The perpetrator may use his courage and strength to face all inner fears – and find his inner source behind them ... the mighty power-magician.

4. the **victim** in the avoidance attitude:

4.1. The life force congestion in the third eye arises from a blockage in the main hair intermediate chakra:
- The victim is unable to move out of his fearful observation of others and his orientation to others (life force congestion in the third eye) into a truly open spiritual encounter with others (crown chakra) – he remains trapped and isolated in his fear.
- The magic of the victim remains stuck in the search for protection.

4.2 The lack of life force in the hara arises from a blockage in the naval intermediate chakra:
- The victim is afraid to take a clear stand and stand firmly on his two feet in the world (activity of the hara) because he fears he will then be attacked – so he blocks his navel intermediate chakra to cut off his hara from life force and become "invisible."
- In magic, the victim is not able to create and represent his own life plan, to form bonds, to separate from others and thus to create his own life.

=> The victim becomes a protection seeking "obedience magician" …

=> Healing: The victim may use the ritual initiation-death – through which he can return again to the heart of life ... the all-releasing initiate.

5. the *addict* in the lack-fixation:

5.1. the life force congestion in the root chakra arises from a blockage in the "gateway to the earth" intermediate chakra:
- The addict is unable to move out of his fixation on getting a particular experience (life force congestion in the root chakra) to a real experience of the world – he remains trapped and isolated in his greed.
- The magic of the addict remains stuck in an eternal, breathless grasping for the supposed fulfillment.

5.2 The lack of life force in the crown chakra arises from a blockage in the main hair intermediate chakra:
- The addict is afraid to look at the world and at the community of all living beings (activity of the crown chakra) because he believes that the others would then take everything away from him – so he closes his main hair intermediate chakra to cut off his parietal chakra from the life force and ultimately remains completely alone in his experience of endless lack.
- In magic, the addict is unable to experience himself as part of the whole and to open himself to the whole so that life can bring him what he would be happy with.

=> The addict becomes a restless "greed-magician" …

=> Healing: The addict can transform his focus on the most longed-for into a spontaneous life as an improvised dance in the here and now – and thus getting a feeling for the self-dynamics of life again ... the concept-free chaos-magician.

6. The **ascetic** in lack-displacement:

6.1 Life force congestion in the crown chakra arises from a blockage in the "gateway to heaven" intermediate chakra:
- The ascetic is unable to move from his fixation on achieving membership in a community by following certain rules (life force congestion in the crown chakra) to a real connectedness with the world – he remains trapped and isolated in his renunciation.
- The ascetic's magic remains stuck in the strict adherence to rules that are hostile to life.

6.2 Lack of life force in the root chakra arises from a blockage in the pubic intermediate chakra:
- The ascetic is afraid to look at his abdomen and all his needs (root chakra activity) because he fears that this would lead him astray from the "right path" – so he closes his pubic hair intermediate chakra so as not to become aware of his great deficiency (root chakra).
- In magic, the ascetic is not able to see, accept and fulfill his own needs.

=> The ascetic becomes an intolerant "do-gooder magician" …

=> Healing: The ascetic can use his rigidity and discipine for regular meditation – through which he can steer the water of life back to its original path ... the one-pointed yogi.

- - -

This somewhat more detailed presentation of the effect of blocked intermediate chakras clearly shows that in magic it is necessary to have open gates between the seven main chakras, otherwise the identity in the heart chakra cannot express itself in the actions and attitudes of the person concerned – which is ultimately the goal of all magic.

Basically there are only two types of disturbance: too loud (addict, perpetrator, star) and too quiet (ascetic, victim, fan). The three aspects of "too loud" or "too quiet" respectively ususally appear together – but with different focus. There is also the possibility of the constant change between these two disturbances (people with a "disorganized attachment").

In the table below, the six polarized magician types shown here are illustrated with the help of characters from the "Harry Potter" series. In addition, there are the three healed mage types and the variant of mage that constantly switches back and forth between the two extremes of a chakra pair.

Some of the listed characters also have characteristics of other polarization types than the type they were listed with.

The Polarization Types in "Harry Potter"				
area	*state*			
	whole	*too loud (congestion in lower chakra)*	*too quiet (congestion in upper chakra)*	*change between too quiet and too loud*
solar plexus + throat chakra (self-love)	self-faithful	star	fan	star/fan
	Harry, Hermine, Cedric	Lockhard, Muriel	Dobby, Doge	Ron
hara + third eye (strength)	in one's own strength	perpetrator	victim	perpetrator/ victim
	Dumbledore, Hagrid, Lily, Krum, Fleur, Mad-Eye	Voldemort, Bellatrix, Umbridge	Wormtail, Neville, Lupin	Severus Snape, Sirius Black, Lucius, Draco, Narcissa
root chakra + crown chakra (abundance)	enjoying	addict	ascetic	addict/ascetic
	Slughorn	Bagman, Dudley	Crouch, Petunia, McGonagal	Fudge, Tonks

II 10. c)   The emergence of a trauma

A trauma is the most intense blockage of an intermediate chakra.
A trauma can occur in a very threatening situation. This process has seven steps:

1. a dangerous situation occurs: Attack by a bear, robbery, rape, crash in the mountains, etc.

2. a spontaneous decision is made as to what is most promising:

a) fight (attack/defense) or

b) escape

If both are not possible or promising, case c) occurs:

c) Surrender

3) If you give up your body, you leave your own body with your consciousness − it has no advantages to witness consciously how you are e.g. eaten by a bear. This is then a near-death experience, an astral journey: The consciousness is outside the body and hovers above it. This is where the motif of the soul bird comes from.

4. If one actually dies, that's it … However, if one survives, the consciousness ("astral body") returns to the body.

5. at this point there are again three possibilities of further development:

a) The person starts to tremble, cry, scream, or the like, thus reducing the hormone adrenaline that has been released in his body by his adrenal glands due to the shock and the highest level of alarm. Then he has returned to the normal state.

b) Someone prevents the person from reducing this adrenaline-filled shock state by trembling, screaming, crying, and the like. Then, an "adrenaline preserve" is created in the body, i.e. a trauma.

c) The person can resolve the state of shock, but the shock experience is repeated several times. As a result, the shock state eventually cannot be resolved anymore because the next dangerous situation is already expected. This is the second possibility of a trauma development.

6. In the "cellar of the psyche", i.e. in the subconscious, there is now a permanent image of the existential threat, which can influence the behavior of the person concerned to a great extent. This "tin-can with this adrenaline reserve in the basement of the psyche" is located on one of the "intermediate chakra shelves" in the basement. This trauma remains as long as it is not specifically resolved – at least no trauma-spontaneous healings seem to be known (but it is also questionable whether such a healing would even be noticed by the medical side).

7. If the person recognizes that he is limited in his actions, he can heal his trauma either by himself or with the help of others.

Trauma healing can be a simple process, but it is a complex process in most cases. It usually has four stages:

1. There is recognition that there is trauma, that is, a blockage of the free flow of the life force in the person's body – in the person's "basement of the psyche" there is a "canned adrenaline" on a shelf, rattling loudly and panicky, putting the whole psyche into a mild state of panic that can become acute at any time. This is the recognition that is the basis of any decision.
This is the "decision".

2. One gradually approaches the trauma by questions, contemplations, dream interpretations, dream journeys, etc., and can finally describe the trauma subject, i.e. the experience that triggered the trauma, quite well. In doing so, the person sees himself in this situation – at the age he had at that time.
This is the "looking."

3. The person approaches the feelings in the trauma. This is often quite difficult and threatening at the first time, but gradually becomes easier. In doing so, it is important to make contact with the feelings locked in the trauma, but at the same time always keep your head above water. Panicking again will not help, only a careful familiarization with the feelings.
This is the "feeling."

4. Finally, the person can go completely into the trauma and embrace himself – that is, the figure of himself that has the age of the time of the origin of the trauma. This is an "embracing" and thus an opening of the tin can and the release of the locked adrenaline, the reintegration of the fear image into one's psyche, the "opening of the tin can on the basement rule".
This is the "embracing".

The three healing steps are "see – feel – embrace", that is "recognize – accept – integrate".

The blockage in one of the intermediate chakras is the "tin can" and the life force congestion that this creates in one of the six outer main chakras is the pressure in this tin can. Due to the fact that (almost) the entire life force of a pair of chakras is dammed up in one of the two affected chakras, a lack of life force occurs in the other chakra of this pair.

Therefore, in another place of the "cellar of the psyche" of the person concerned, one can also find an empty tin can, which evokes the feeling of a constant lack …

It is obvious that such a trauma affects not only the psyche of the subject to a great extent, but also the magic that the subject performs. Trauma can lead to a fixation on a particular subject and also on a particular fear, thereby both impairing and distracting the subject's magic, or even forcing it in the trauma direction altogether.

Moreover, in most cases trauma will also prevent the life force from flowing freely outward from the heart chakra – which is the basic prerequisite for free and effective magic.

Clearing the blockages at the intermediate chakras leads to a significant increase in the effectiveness of magic.

There are two types of trauma, which differ in their effect:

> 1. One type of trauma remains more or less confined to the original fear issue and manifests only when this issue arises in the life of the person concerned. The subject will then have difficulties only in magical undertakings related to this subject.

> 2. The other kind of trauma expands more and more and draws more and more subjects into the "fear circle": the rattling of the one adrenaline can on the shelf in the cellar of the psyche gradually causes everything else that is in that cellar to rattle as well. This general state of unrest can extend to the point of the person's inability to act – which, of course, will also massively limit the effectiveness of that person's magic.

These two possibilities are, of course, only the two extreme variants. They are the most common, but there are of course also variants that lie in between and in which the entire psyche is not constantly "rattling" and "runs on adrenalin", but in which the trauma panic has merely extended to two or three other issues.

II 11. Summary: The Three-Step

Now that the Three-Step has been considered in some detail, one can describe its individual aspects in more detail. These aspects are:

1. inside (source, consciousness, deep sleep state, heart chakra)

    - transition 1 (wish tree and thymus intermediate chakra)

2. phase 1 (solar plexus, throat chakra)

    - transition 2 (navel and palate intermediate chakra)

3. phase 2 (hara, third eye)

    - transition 3 (pubic and main hair intermediate chakra)

4. phase 3 (root chakra, crown chakra)

    - transition 4 (gateway to earth, gateway to heaven)

5. outside (matter)

In addition, there are two more aspects:

6. development

7. specifics

Inside
(heart chakra)

Consciousness
Here is found pure consciousness, that is, consciousness without content, to which one returns in deep sleep and in silent meditation. This is the inside of the world, which is of course connected to its outside at every point, but here only the inside is considered. In the big picture, this consciousness is the One God.

Matter
This inside is the singularity before the Big Bang.

Transition 1 (wish tree and thymus intermediate chakra)

Consciousness

Here the identity is concretized into impulses. The first of these concretizations is the incarnation of the soul at the procreation of its body by its future parents. Here everything happens at once – incarnation or not incarnation (there is no "half incarnation").

In the big picture, it is at this transition that the many deities arise from the One God. This transition is also called the "First Cause".

Matter

This corresponds to the Big Bang and the violent expansion of the universe right after the Big Bang ("inflationary universe").

Phase 1
(solar plexus and throat chakra)

Consciousness

In phase 1 everything is interconnected and acts unrestrictedly and without restraint. Therefore, this state is unified and stable. In this consciousness all contents are equal – everything is visible and everything works.

Everything is a part of the I, everything is filled with self-love and related to its origin in one's own soul in the heart chakra – a perfect expression of the soul. This area is completely inner-determined and completely independent of the outside. It is soul-centered.

This state is creative, it is a wanting, a concentration, a pre-joy – the state of an omnipotent king in his domain.

Here is found an unrestrained self-affirmation.

This is the subconscious (Tree of Life: Yesod) with the individual images, that is part of the collective subconscious (Tree of Life: Da'ath) with the archetypes (deities). This area is without boundaries – everything is connected to each other bey tlepathy and telekinesis. This connectedness and boundlessness is a certain quality of the area of the deities.

The "3" symbolizes self-expression in organic form.

The "6" symbolizes a group of like-minded people and allies – it is a helper of the "3".

Matter

In this phase the universe consists only of light, which can move completely unhindered, because there is still no matter, which could influence the light.

This is the physical side of the boundlessness of the deities.

Transition 2
(navel and palate intermediate chakra)

Consciousness

Here the concrete desires of phase 2 arise from the general desires of phase 1. This is only possible as long as the intensity of the impulses is great enough.

In the big picture, at this transition many souls arise from the deities, which are, so to speak, "drops from the sea of a deity". This transition is also called "abyss".

Matter

In the origin of the universe this corresponds to the compression and encapsulation of the energy to matter. This is only possible as long as after the big bang the energy density in the universe is still big enough.

Phase 2
(hara and third eye)

Consciousness

Phase 2 is less stable than phase 1, because it is formed both from the inside and from the outside. Here the impulses coming from the soul (phase 1) are concretized on the basis of the possibilities in the world – which is why these concretizations will also change again and again.

In this state contents are selected, which are taken up into the consciousness – those, which are of importance for the momentary situation. This is the waking consciousness.

One accepts and rejects, one says "yes" and says "no". Here we find a differentiated evaluation of all things – and a corresponding action. Since it is about implementing what one chooses, "strength" is the central concept here – in addition to the clarity needed to recognize the situation.

Situations are shaped and sustainable structures are created. One recovers pleasant things and proven strategies. By the success achieved in this way, joy is created.

This creative shaping also extends to the effecting of magic.

The "2" symbolizes the complementary opposition and the rhythm.

The "4" symbolizes space, freedom and distinct forms – it is a helper of the "2".

Matter

In this phase the universe is, so to speak, still one big sun, in which matter and energy (light) are completely equally distributed – it is everywhere equally dense, hot and bright, but is a mixture of light (energy) and atomic nuclei (matter).

This is the physical side of the general possibilities (energy) and the dicisions that one has made (matter).

Transition 3
(pubic hair and main hair intermediate chakra)

Consciousness

Here the concrete desires become concrete actions and thus concrete experiences. There are alternating processes here – activity and rest.

In the big picture, the psyche arises from the soul at this transition. This transition is also called "trench".

Matter

At this transition a different distribution of the light in the universe arises as well as the atoms with an electron shell.

Phase 3
(root chakra and crown chakra)

Consciousness

In phase 3 everything is directed towards a single point: the one-pointed presence in the here and now. This phase is the least stable or steady, as it always refers to the moment – this phase is characterized by great mobility.

This is the state of ecstasy – one-pointedness.

Here the consciousness has only one content and can therefore reach the state of ecstasy. One agrees with the situation and enjoys the moment. By this one is connected with what is there – one lives in fullness. One is in contact with the world, one is associated with it, one experiences commonality.

In doing so, one shapes from within what is outside.

The "1" symbolizes centering, unambiguity and unity.

The "5" symbolizes order, healthy tension and healing – it is a helper of the "1".

Matter

In the evolution of the universe the thermal equilibrium ends here, thus the homogeneous condition of the one "sun", which fills the entire universe – atoms develop, which unite to galaxies, stars, planets and moons and between them empty space.

Transition 4
("gate to the earth" and "gate to the sky")

Consciousness

This is the contact to the outside, the acting on matter – both physically by the senses and the limbs and magically by telepathy and telekinesis.

This transition takes place only when the motivation has become high enough and "one-pointed".

On the whole, at this transition from the psyche the physical body arises, respectively the body is shaped by the psyche (e.g. emergence of diseases and their healing). This transition is also called "threshold". The psyche has an effect in the material world only when it "brings a thing to the point".

Matter

This is the condensation of matter to the critical point where the "stability" of the atoms can no longer withstand the huge gravity of the great accumulation of matter (giant stars).

This transition can take place only if in a galaxy center a sufficient matter density is present. This condition must be reached first. Then the whole matter concerned (a giant sun) condenses to almost a point.

Außen
(matter)
Consciousness
Here only the matter without consciousness is found, thus only the outside of the world. Of course, it is connected at every point with its inside, but here only the material outside is considered.
Matter
In the evolution of the universe now so much matter has accumulated in the centers of the galaxies that black holes can develop from them, in which the entire matter contained in them collapses to almost a single point.

The transitions in general

At the transitions new forms arise – if in the area preceding it prevails a sufficiently high intensity. At the 1st transition this is always the case, at the 2nd transition only for a certain time, at the 3rd transition this changes rhythmically, and at the 4th transition this intensity must be reached always anew.

At the transitions the identity is concretized from the inside to the outside, whereby in each case a part of the freedom is lost, but in return the intensity and the unambiguity increases.

The four transitions in the chakra system (intermediate chakras) are identical with the four transitions on the Tree of Life (First Cause, Abyss, Trench, Threshold) – both systems are based on the three-step, i.e. on the sequence of the three phases.

The new forms have inside and outside the form of a twelve-divided circle – inside the astrological zodiac and outside the superstring.

The "12" symbolizes the next step in each case, the next development and transformation, and the flow of life.

The intermediate chakras are the places in the chakra system that are also most important for magic.

Identity unfolds in three phases, which have different qualities. The first phase of unrestrained self-love is always the support – and phase 1 again rests in identity, which is simply what it is.

The path from inside to outside begins with a perfect self-centeredness (phase 1) and develops through the meeting of inside and outside (phase 2) to a perfect presence in the world (phase 3). Therefore, phase 1 is always the same (as it relates to identity), while phase 2 gradually develops according to the acquaintance with the world and the possibilities it currently offers – finally, in phase 3, the experience of the world is found, i.e. a distinct world-relatedness and thus a constant change.

Phase 1 contains all contents of consciousness, phase 2 those which are relevant in the moment and phase 3 only one content: the momentary experiencing. This can be understood as an increasing restriction of attention to a single thing on the outside. In this process, structure, orientation, concreteness, closeness to the world, and experiencing the outside increasingly emerge.

From 'Phase 1' towards 'Phase 3' there are four developments in total:

- The speed of movement decreases from the speed of light over a small speed to "0". => The intensity and the degree of freedom decreases – also in the psyche.

- The solidity increases from "formless" over "formed" to "point-like". => Things become more concrete – also in the psyche.

- Size shrinks from "vastness" to "limitedness" to "point". => Things become smaller – also in the psyche.

- The mass increases from "tiny" over "normal" to "almost endless". => Things become more effective – also in the psyche.

- The consciousness includes less and less things and becomes more and more intensive for it. => The things are perceived more intensively – also in the psyche.

This process creates a space in which one moves, as well as social organisms in which one participates.

This is a process of creation, a magical action. The greatest possible hindrance in this process is the creation of a trauma, that is, the blockage of an intermediate chakra, i.e. a "life force spasm".

The exercise of the Middle Pillar serves to strengthen one's radiation, i.e. this concretization process. This also concretizes the identity in the heart chakra in a more intense and prominent way.

Special features

On the Tree of Life and in the Superstring Theory, the 3 phases have each been subdivided once again into 3 subphases, so that together with "inside" and "outside" there are eleven areas.

Many three-step systems have two directions: Tummo and Bindhu, Lightning and Snake, Big Bang and Energy/Matter/Black Hole, Birth and Death, Snake and Eagle, Creation and Realization …

Since all things can be represented as a tree of life, all things also contain a three-step in them.

III   The Application of the Three-Step in Magic

Now that the three-step has been considered and fundamentally characterized, it can be applied specifically to magic.

III 1.   The Healing of the Chakras

Since magic consists of the consciousness having a material effect, it is of fundamental importance for magic to dissolve and heal possible blockages and traumas in the intermediate chakras, as well as fear, addiction and deficiency in the six main outer chakras.

III 1. a)   Chakra meditations

The simplest and most undifferentiated method of chakra healing is the following meditation:

- while inhaling:
    - imagine inhaling light and directing it into the chosen chakra
    - inwardly speak "life"

- while exhaling:
    - imagine that the light is shining in the chosen chakra
    - inwardly speak "life"

One can also speak the name of a deity or one's own soul while inhaling – this is then a request to this deity or to one's own soul to send light (life force).

While breathing out, one can also speak a word internally that describes the healing state of the chakra in question. The list below contains suggestions for such a specialized chakra mantra. Of course, one can also use the classical chakra mantras from yoga.

122

Chakra-Mantras		
chakra	*mantra-suggestion*	*classic mantra*
crown chakra	God – light	ang
third eye	Horus – will	aum
throat chakra	Athena – self-expression	ham
heart chakra	Osiris – love	yam
solar plexus	Helios – radiation	ram
hara	Inanna – support	vam
root chakra	Ymir – life	lam

III 1. b)   Heart meditation

Heart meditation is a meditation by which one finds contact with one's own soul. There are instructions for this experience in almost every religion – from the dream journey to one's own center, to the vision quest, to the mystery cults.

The simplest form is the mantra meditation with the two words "soul – love". The dream journey to one's own center is also very helpful. A third form, which is an important addition to these two variants, is the silence meditation (Zen), in which one is only a consciousness without content – one is just consciousness that is aware of itself.

Silence is the substance of the soul – the experiences on the dream journey to the center are the image of the soul and the heart meditation is the anchoring of the soul in everyday life.

In heart meditation it is important that after a while one really longs to find one's own soul and to live it – without the feeling nothing really gets going … only the image or the concept is not enough (there is then the 'phase 1' missing).

III 1. c)   The awakening of Kundalini

The awakening of the Kundalini is also a rather complex subject. The simplest form for this is the mantra "fire – fire" and the imagination of a small fiery red glowing cone in the root chakra with its tip pointing upwards.

123

Heart meditation promotes the radiance of the soul and is similar to the central control of the body by the brain.

Kundalini meditation connects all parts of the vital force body and is comparable to the circulation of blood.

III 1. d) The individual chakra healing

Such a complex subject, involving the entire psyche and also the horoscope, can of course not be analyzed in a short book "for beginners". Although there are some elements that will quite certainly appear on any healing path, such as the perception of the chakras or the healing of possibly existing traumas, in the end everyone has to find his or her individual path.

III 2.   A Single Magical Act

One can now consider a single magical action. What steps does it have? What is the significance of each step? What should one pay attention to?

III 2. a)   Identity (source)

Ideally, the root of a magical action lies in one's own identity, that is, in what one really is – in one's own soul, in the stillness of consciousness in the heart chakra, which has no content, but is aware of itself.

At the entrance to the Oracle of Delphi there were two sayings: "Know thyself." and "Nothing in excess." The first saying refers to the soul, the second to the avoidance or dissolution of all polarization extremes in the psyche.

Whether a magical action ultimately springs from the heart chakra or not can be easily determined: If the magical action succeeds and one can enjoy its fruits, it has had roots reaching into the heart chakra …

Concentration on the heart chakra is the attitude of the yogi.

III 2. b)   General desire (phase 1)

The second step is also in magic the general desire. This appears in magic as the feeling, the need, the motivation that leads to a high concentration on the goal.

If you have to strain to concentrate on imagining the goal, there is something wrong with the goal. When the desired goal is firmly anchored in the heart chakra, concentration on the goal and imagination of the goal comes easily – it would be rather difficult not to strive for it.

However, fixation on a polarized extreme also leads to high concentration and constant imagination. However, this single-mindedness has something obsessive about it and is accompanied by feelings of lack (polarization in phase 3), fear (polarization in phase 2), or self-doubt (polarization in phase 1).

To clear the general desire, it helps to take a step back and do the silence meditation several times.

Concentrating on phase 1 is the attitude of the dancer and the singer.

III 2. c)   Concrete wish (phase 2)

One can have two types of concrete wishes in magic:

    In the one case, the concreteness consists merely in wanting to have a certain kind of experience (to find a relationship, more money, health, etc.).

    In the second case, the concretization goes much further and the relationship with a certain person is wanted, the money is wanted in a certain way, one wants to get healthy in a very concrete way, etc.

    In this second case, the obstacles are greater: Does the other person want to have a relationship with you at all? Is there actually enough money in the source from which one wants to become rich? Does one's own body actually need what one imagines for oneself to be healthy?

    There may be conflicts with other people who want something different, or with circumstances that make the fulfillment of the magical wish difficult.

    So possibly "fighting magic" is needed, which asserts itself against the will of others. The question, however, is whether this will ultimately get you what you want – and whether you will get it in a way you can enjoy.

Concretization has another aspect: by concretizing, one gives form to the general desire, one establishes a point in time – one grounds the general desire.

This giving of form contains in many forms of magic also the aspect of the selection of analogies, which are to strengthen the desire. This is not absolutely necessary, but quite helpful. These analogies, which may appear as a talisman, a ritual structure, a symbol, an invoked deity, etc., should correspond as closely as possible to the goal one is pursuing.

However, this form may well be reduced to the decision that one wants something now. In this, the conviction that one is doing exactly the right thing, that the magical action is exactly what one wants, is the form that the magical action needs.

This sense of purpose, determination and rightness ultimately arise from the heart chakra: one allows what one is to become the action and the attitude. When one's identity can flow freely as a general desire through Phase 1, then not much form is needed in Phase 2 – then it is enough to say what one wants … or simply to act. When this free flowing is achieved, magic becomes very simple and at the same time very effective. Then "ordinary magic" may become "extraordinary magic", i.e. "miracles" like materializations, levitations, transformations of objects and the like.

Focusing on phase 2 is the attitude of the hunter and the warrior.

III 2. d)   Here and Now (phase 3)

This phase is the grounding. This is often just a small gesture or word that is not hardly noticeable at first – the Amen in church, the "Ho!" in the sweat lodge, the Kabbalistic cross at the end of a ritual, the touching of the earth with the tip of the right index finger by Buddha Akshobhya, and so on.

This gesture or word is small but essential – it says "here" and "now" and "yes" – it is the dot at the end of the sentence, the signature under what has been said.

Sometimes this grounding is also the doing itself, as for example in combat magic, where there are no rituals, but only the doing itself.

This "magical signature" should be sincere, otherwise there will be problems. If something feels strange about it, you should read the draft for the magical action again carefully before you "sign" it. This "draft" is the form you created in Phase 2. If correcting this form makes one feel good again, it is ok – if this is not enough, one should return to the feelings in phase 1 or even completely to the source in the heart chakra.

Concentrating on phase 3 is the attitude of the child and the enjoyer.

III 3.   Forms of Magic and their Relation to the Three-Step

There are many different forms of magic. They differ, among other things, in which of the three phases they emphasize.

III 3. a) Source

The heart chakra is the focus of only a few forms of magic, although this is an effective form of magic – but just a very undramatic one.

Heart Chakra Magic

The magicians who have chosen the heart chakra as the focus of their magic hardly ever appear as magicians, because they themselves hardly ever purposefully actively shape their life circumstances. They rest in themselves and are sure of themselves and radiate this into the world, which then shapes itself in such a way that it corresponds to what these magicians are and what they want to experience.

One can take the standpoint that this is no longer magic, as well as the standpoint that this is the only really effective kind of magic. To the one who behaves in this way, this question will probably be quite meaningless …

Taoism

In Taoism there is first the flow of life: the "Tao".

Second, there is the "non-doing" as the meaningful behavior: the "Wu-Wei. This means that one does not go against life – and not against one's own truth.

This behavior creates a magical effect, a harmony between oneself and the world and life: the "Tê".

Apart from Lao-tse and Chuang-tse themselves, from whom the form of Taoism known today descends, there have been some more famous figures in more recent times who have strong Taoist traits. These are mainly "Mister Miyagi" from "The Karate Kid" and "Master Yoda" from "Star-Wars". Interestingly, some animals in comics such as the dog "Snoopy" or the fantasy creature "Marsupilami" also have a distinct Taoist character.

III 3. b)   Phase 1

Phase 1 is characterized by egocentricity, selfishness, self-centeredness, self-love, and so on: One is totally focused on what one wants to express in one's life.

This is the magic of the solar plexus and the throat chakra.

If there is a problem in this "phase of self-love", self-doubt arises, and as a result, the "star" and the "fan" arise.

Invocation

A typical element of this phase is the invocation of a deity, a spirit, a demon, one's own soul, etc. However, this does not mean a traditional, formal and matter-of-fact recitation of a text, but a fervent prayer, an imploring petition, an ecstatic identification with a deity (invocation), and so on.

For this form of intense feelings and complete single-mindedness of motivation, there is the beautiful, ancient term "to inflame oneself with prayer".

This form of magic by an invocation is sometimes called "theurgy", when the person considers the effect of the magic as the act of a deity and not his own act.

Evocations

Evocation, i.e. the calling of a spirit, is a method of obtaining sufficient intensity or life force with which one can then magically realize one's own desire.

With an invocation you call a deity, a spirit or a ghost into yourself – with an evocation you call a deity, a spirit or a ghost in front of yourself.

The oldest variant of this procedure is the calling of ancestral spirits from their grave or mound. This procedure has been somewhat discredited by the Christian church – the associations with "necromancy" are not the best today. However, this effective method is beginning to re-establish itself under the name of "systemic family constellations".

The most notorious variant is the "pact with the devil", which is also a Christian reinterpretation of seeking help from ancestral spirits. In any case, summoning the devil or a demon is at least an excellent aid to concentration …

Sigil Magic

The core of sigil magic is the short, violent concentration on the sigil, that is, the feelings of phase 1. The sigil is a newly created sign that expresses the wish that you want to fulfill with this form of magic.

Chaos Magic

The basis of chaos magic is the assumption that there is no "right" and no "wrong" and thus ultimately no knowledge, but only the will of the one who performs magic. The worldview therefore becomes something arbitrary – one always uses the world-view that suits one best at the moment. Here, too, the will of the magician and thus phase 1 is in the foreground. The shaping of phase 2 is completely subordinated to the will of the magician.

Ice magic

The ice magic designed by Frater U.D. goes one step further and cathegorically focuses on the will of the magician. By this view, the magician ultimately becomes the creator of his own world.

Miracles

This attitude also exists with many religion founders, saints and the like persons. As a rule, however, they do not place their own will in the center of their single-mindedness, but a deity – the exception is Buddha, who rejects any deities as a goal or as points of orientation.

This thorough single-mindedness makes it possible to perform not only "ordinary magic" but also miracles.

Forgetting

Forgetting plays an important role in magic: when one has sent out a wish (e.g. with the help of a sigil), one intentionally forgets the entire magical action. This serves to avoid disturbing the effect of the magical action by thoughts, doubts and the like.

One avoids, so to speak, disturbances in phase 2, which could disturb the realization of the magical wish from phase 1 – thoughts, doubts and all kinds of forms belong to phase 2.

Trust

The alternative to forgetting is trusting. If one trusts completely in the deity whom one has asked for the fulfillment of a wish, there will be no disturbance of the wish fulfillment – one believes unshakably in the fulfillment of the wish.

This is what is meant when Jesus said that faith can move mountains. Such a firm faith is a permanent one-pointedness.

Faith, once acquired, has the advantage that it can lead to consistent wish fulfillment. Especially in smaller communities of faith like the Jesus-People, the Krishna-Disciples etc. this kind of trust is used to regulate daily life – in the morning they wish together for the things they need, pray for them – and in the evening they have received them all from somebody. Of course, this may be done not only in a group, but also alone.

Causeless joy

Trust can become a general anticipation of the fulfillment of one's wishes. A friend of mine once described her attitude toward life with the words, "I look forward to what is coming." This is the extreme case of confidence, so to speak.

You can write yourself a wish list with all the things you would like to have. Next, you try to wish really completely unrestrained and then complete the wish list with the additional wishes – to be able to fly, to be able to be invisible, to drink tea with the Dalai Lama, to play a round of chess with Caesar … whatever …

Afterwards, one can then read this wish list aloud with the idea that all these wishes have come true. This creates a great joy that radiates from the inside out.

This joy does not need the desired event to arise – this joy is already there and in turn wants the event to arise. This joy is not the consequence of the wish fulfillment, but the cause of the wishes, in which this joy can then express and experience itself.

From this can arise a constant radiance - the essence of phase 1 …

III 3. c)   Phase 2

Phase 2 is characterized by form, analogies, strength and possibly also struggles: One encounters the world, one uses it, one shapes it, one fights with opponents, one becomes more and more concrete with one's desires and intentions.

This is the magic of the hara and the third eye.

If there is a problem in this "phase of strength", might (power over something) arises instead of strength (power for something) and so does the "perpetrator" and the "victim".

Talisman magic

The forms of magic that emphasize Phase 2 are much more formal and are often based on traditions. They assume, unlike the "phase 1" forms of magic, that there is always a "right" and a "wrong".

In talismanic magic, the core is the making of an object according to a traditional magical point of view – just a talisman. Quite popular are the talismans oriented to astrology – a Mars talisman (e.g. for more power in combat or for more sex) could be, for example, a pentagon of iron, made on a Tuesday, on which the Mars symbol, the Mars seal, the name of the Mars archangel Samael, etc. has been engraved and consecrated with blood.

There is consecration in talismans as well, but it is generally considered that the proper making of the talisman has the greatest part in the effect.

One should not underestimate this aspect of magic either: If one uses symbols in magic, the actual symbolism will also prevail – even if one should have misinterpreted the symbol. The symbol is stronger than one's own imagination about the symbol and thus one's imagination during the consecration.

In the magic methods that focus on phase 1, almost no symbols are used.

Astrological magic

In astrological magic, the rituals are very much oriented to the current planets' positions – not only the preference for full moon nights, but also the positions of the other planets are taken into account.

As sources of power in the rituals the planets are logically used above all – possibly they are invoked with the help of the planetary hexagrams from the tradition of the Golden Dawn.

Cult

A cult consists of regular rituals, which in most cases are meant to promote the well-being of a whole community. The effect of such rituals is usually attributed to the deities invoked – the priest or priestess who leads these rituals plays only a minor role in the effectiveness of the rituals. The magic in the cult is thus primarily a theurgy, i.e. a "deity-magic".

This form of magic is set against the background of a particular religion and it is effective because of a formally correct action. It is the form of magic that most emphasizes phase 2.

Informal wishing

The book "The Cosmic Ordering Service" by Barbel Mohr has (re)made known another form of magic. The "universe" has taken the place of the gods – this image of the "cosmic department store" ties in with orders placed with mail-order companies and on the Internet, which evokes a familiarity with the process even among non-magicians.

Here it is simply the expressed wish that has the effect – that is, an informal order. This is done without any concentration, imagination, invocation of deities, etc.

Repetitions

There is also a kind of "unwanted magic" in connection with Phase 2: repetition. Forms, once imprinted, tend to repeat themselves, which is known, among other things, from psychology as the "repetition compulsion" and from astrology as a person's horoscope, which is effective throughout life.

These repetitions can be, for example, on the type of relationships, the type of jobs, the type of living situations or similar experiences and life circumstances. However, they can also occur in small details such as names of people with whom one has a particular relationship.

(For example, I had a best female friend several times in a row who all had the same name – and also a man with the same name, so always e.g. "Anna and Josef". My ex-wife had the same name as my oldest sister, etc.).

There are obviously imprints in the phase 2, which are effective, although these imprints are not wanted by the magician. These imprints occur even in the strongest magicians – they are, so to speak, "life themes".

III 3. d)　Phase 3

Phase 3 is characterized by the presence in the here and now and thus also by the willingness to get involved in the rhythm of life: One is fully where one is and fully with what one is doing – grounding one's magical action.

This is the magic of the root chakra and the crown chakra.

If there is a problem in this "phase of abundance", lack arises, and so do the "addict" and the "ascetic".

Being in the moment

The "Be here now!" is rarely found as the basis of magic – strictly speaking, however, the magical effect of this attitude is rarely called magic, although it is certainly present.

This attitude has similarity with the heart chakra magic, because the consistent presence in the here and now leads to the fact that one also becomes more and more conscious of oneself.

In addition, this attitude also connects the person concerned with the "flow of life", i.e. with the collective subconsciousness and thus also with the gods (archetypes).

In Taoism, both "relaxing into the here and now," as so beautifully formulated by Mahasiddhi Maitrepa, and "acting from one's own truth" are recommended.

III 4.   The Systematic Application of the Three-Step Approach

One may see now if, based on all these considerations, one can develop a systematic (and effective) use of the three-step. However, the intended model should leave enough room for a different emphasis on the three phases and the heart chakra to make it suitable for different types of magicians and sorceresses.

III 4. a)   The foundation: heart chakra

This part is simple and difficult at the same time – it is the sincerely asked and answered question "Who am I?"

If this question cannot be truly answered honestly and accurately, the magical action will not result in a state that can be enjoyed.

III 4. b)   The 1ˢᵗ step: solar plexus and throat chakra

This part follows from the previous one: "What do I want?" The answer to this question should be sought completely uninfluenced by external circumstances. If one should want to fly like a bird, then this is just the thing one wants – regardless of whether one can achieve it or not. This desire to fly should not be suppressed because it is unrealizable – if it is true, it is an expression of what one is.

The activities that express this phase most directly are improvised music-making and dancing, wandering, playing, and the like.

The answers to the two questions "Who am I?" and "What do I want?" show where one stands and where one wants to go. In this impulse lies the power that gives the magical action its effectiveness.

III 4. c)   The 2ⁿᵈ step: hara and third eye

This part also follows from the previous one: "How do I want to make this happen?" Here the "What do I want?" becomes concrete. You develop a plan, decide on specific steps and methods, and take concrete steps.

Depending on the style of magic one uses, this part takes up quite little or a lot of space.

Here the attitude of a hunter or warrior is needed, who knows exactly what he wants, who pursues his goal clearly and single-mindedly, and who asserts himself.

III 4. d)   The 3rd step: root chakra and crown chakra

Again, this part follows from the previous one – it is the beginning of the magical action and it is the final point at its end: the signature that grounds the whole.

III 5. The Widening of the Three-Step

The three-step has so far been widely considered as the action of a single magician or sorceress. Often, however, a magical action stands in larger contexts, which should be considered as well.

III 5. a) Deep sleep consciousness
(heart chakra)

The stillness in the heart chakra, i.e., the deep sleep consciousness, is in the broadest sense of this realm the consciousness as the inside of the whole world, i.e., God.

The more one is anchored in this realm, the more effective one's magic becomes. Of course, this does not mean submissiveness to God, but only unconditional loyalty to oneself.

=> This realm is always a unity.

III 5. b) Subconsciousness
(solar plexus and throat chakra)

The individual subconsciousbess is a part of the collective subconscious, which consists of the totality of all subconsciousnesses – or in other words, of the totality of the life force. This is the realm of telepathy and telekinesis, and thus the most important realm of magic – this is the realm of boundlessness. In it magic happens – no matter whether one includes this area consciously or not.

=> In this area all things are connected with each other.

III 5. c) Waking consciousness
(hara and third eye)

Magic is often practiced by a group of people: a witchcraft coven, a spiritualist session, a magician's order, a congregation, a druid's covenant, a yogi's retinue, and so on. At the same time, the people in such a group are usually coordinated with each other in a waking consciousness by their coinciding intentions and views.

=> In this realm, things can be mutually supportive.

III 5. d) Ecstasy
(root chakra and crown chakra)

The grounding of magic is done by one's own decision, but it is of course possible to do it together with several presons – like the "Amen" in church.
However, the one-pointedness must be achieved by everyone for himself, even if of course several people can be one-pointed at the same time.

=> In this area, things can promote each other, but the state of ecstasy must be reached by each person.

III 6. The Experience of the Source and the Three Steps

The Source and the Three Step are not only aspects of a magical action, but fundamentally four different aspects of the psyche. As such, they also contain different states of consciousness, feelings, experiences, and so on. These experiences make the essence of these four aspects of the psyche really clear and they also make it possible to consider these aspects in magic. Therefore, the concrete own experience of these four aspects is also extremely important – what one does not know, one can hardly use.

Now, the experiences that belong to these four aspects can be described and also the possible way to them, but you have to find and experience them yourself.

A general problem is that words can express qualities and structures, but not the depth in which a sentence is meant and also not the intensity of the experience one describes.

III 6. a)   The Source
(heart chakra)

The simplest form in which one can experience the heart chakra is its physical perception as a "beginning to glow": the awakening of the heart chakra. This really means a physical perception – it feels as if a fire is glowing in the center of the chest.

This fire is filled with love, which is not directed at anything in particular and which is at the same time a deep happiness. One can reach this experience, for example, by a heart meditation (mantra meditation, breath guidance, prayer to a deity).

The "going into silence" is clearly different in approach, but ultimately leads to the same experience – you sit there and smile like Buddha to yourself … and the smile gets wider and wider until you start "to grin like a Cheshire cat".

Both experiences have in common that they don't need any external circumstances for the "glowing happiness" – they take place in the "consciousness itself", thus in the "consciousness without consciousness contents".

One can also perform the "dream journey to one's own center" and thereby meet one's own soul. This can also be a very moving experience – one suddenly sees who one is in front of oneself and recognizes directly that this is so. At this moment, for example, the question of the meaning of life also ceases, because one sees one's own

meaning of life standing before one: The meaning of life is to express what one is –
and the essence of what one is is one's soul.

There is a completely other approach to reaching this state: doing nothing. If you
observe animals, you will find that they often just stand there or sit there and do
nothing. They are awake and present, but completely relaxed and are just there …
This "normal zero" state corresponds to empty consciousness, that is, deep sleep
consciousness, which is connected to waking consciousness: inner silence.
You can practice this state and just sit down and see if you need anything right now
– really need it right now at this moment. If not, you just stay sitting … This sounds
extremely simple, but it is also extremely effective … you start to let go …
This in turn has the effect of allowing the things you have otherwise longed for to
finally come to you – doing nothing gives life the space to be there … Doing nothing
is one of the most creative things you can do.

All these methods lead to the feeling of being fulfilled: one is present in oneself, one
feels one's own soul, one lives …

III 6. b) Phase 1
(solar plexus and throat chakra)

The feeling of this phase is the natural and self-evident self-centeredness and self-
expression. Basically, all the words with "self-", "I-" and "ego-" belong here, since
these two chakras contain what the soul wants to be in its present incarnation.

Therefore, when one goes to this area, one feels an unobstructed, unrestricted
radiance. One can also call this area the will – in the sense of a force that is directed
towards what one likes. This inner pressure is the experience of complete autonomy –
it is like an "all-around laser beam" emanating from the heart chakra. This area is the
intentional expansion of the heart chakra into the world, the song of the center, the
dance of the soul, the radiance of the inner sun …
As with the solar wind, there is only one source in this area: the soul. And there is
also only one direction: into the world. However, this realm is completely unaffected
by what is possible in the world and what is going on in it right now. If one wants to
love, one loves. If one wants to fly, one wants to fly. If you want to become wise, you
want to become wise. That's just the way it is. It's not a question of possibilities,
opportunity, realism, reason and things like that … it just is. Basta!

Therein lies also an anticipation – which does not depend on what one can realistically achieve, but which simply refers to the fact that one wants to achieve it. This anticipation is a result of self-fidelity. I want. Period.

This state is the "I am I" in action. There is a great power in this radiance – it is ultimately without limits … at least when viewed from within, since there is nothing to limit it – it is simply what one wants, and that is the only thing to which one aligns one's power. I want – and that with all my power … without any "if" and "but".

This clear alignment, this flowing out of the heart chakra as the only source, this unquestioning independence can be experienced as "electrically sparkling heat" in the solar plexus and as "tingling radiant warmth" in the throat chakra.

III 6. c) Phase 2
(hara and third eye)

In this area, the inner meets the outer. Here the radiance from phase 1 becomes the structures of phase 2.

Here again one can experience the chakras: the "rotating warmth" in the hara and the "warm pulsating pressure" in the third eye. The hara gives an inner support to one's own position and the third eye gives orientation.

In this area the general wanting becomes specific wanting – the general desires become concrete desires. The first stage of concretization consists simply in wanting something now – and not just sometime. The second stage of concretization consists in making a choice and wanting to do something with a particular person, in a particular place, in a particular way, and so on.

While the first stage of concretization is still almost always feasible, there can be difficulties with the second stage. Therefore, one may sometimes have to let go of something, change plans, need a new concept, etc. If, even in the second concretization stage of phase 2, one is oriented only to what one wants, it is possible that one will lose touch with reality.

However, one should not make the mistake of "switching off" phase 1 when meeting an obstacle. Magic is also about doing the impossible. Therefore, in phase 2 a sure instinct is needed for which obstacle in the outside shows you that another way would be better (e.g. letting go of a deceased person), and which obstacle can be dissolved by magic (where you just "move mountains with your faith" if necessary).

141

In this area, the impulses from phase 1 in the encounter with the world become a foundation, supporting bones, a protective shell, defensible horns, claws and teeth. Phase 2 gives firmness and determination.

III 6. d) Phase 3
(root chakra and crown chakra)

The perception in the root chakra has at least four stages:

     1. a pleasant, diffuse heat

     2. an electric tingling sensation that spreads upward, especially on the outside of the body

     3. a "heat envelope" around the body

     4. an intense ball of "fire-pressure" that slowly rises in the center of the body ("with the speed of a crawling turtle"), expanding into a rod that eventually reaches from the root chakra to the crown chakra ("kundalini snake")

In the crown chakra, there is a feeling that the scalp arches upward and begins to glisten and tingle slightly.

In this area you are simply where you are. However, after a while this has a great effect: this simply being there leads to feeling life in everything and to "seeing without form" life in everything. It is more a knowing than a visual seeing, but this knowing is not abstract at all, but very direct. By this perception, one may be filled with a causeless happiness and a deep love that is not related to anything concrete. Then the heart chakra has arrived in the world …
  There may be certain places or circumstances that facilitate finding this state – probably they vary from person to person. Sometimes it is the light of the setting sun on the bark of a tree, sometimes it is simply the sight of a blade of grass, a flower or the sunset … the triggers are things in nature rather than man-made things. Sometimes it is places where one has experienced something beautiful or important …

It is a being-present by which one is completely satisfied and filled with an objectless abundance …

III 7. The Overall Gesture

The overall gesture created by the source and the three phases, although clear and concise, is difficult to describe: One lives – and lives the right way and totally!

One is oneself and radiates and creates out of oneself an environment that reflects one's own truth and enjoys the creating and the created.

It is a flow:

> silence – singing – speaking – exclamation

or:

> body – dance – work – sex

or:

> yogi – dancer – warrior – epicure

or:

> Buddha – singer – hunter – experiencer

It is a radiance from the heart that takes shape in the world and that can be enjoyed wholeheartedly …

This is magic.

English Books by Harry Eilenstein

- Living Magic (261 p.)
- The Synthesis of Physics and Magic (192 p.)
- Telepathy for Beginners (60 p.)
- Telepathy for Advanced Learners (52 p.)
- Telekinesis for Beginners (56 p.)
- Life Force for Beginners (76 p.)
- Astral Projection for Beginners (60 p.)
- Meditation for Beginners (60 p.)
- Prophecy for Beginners (60 p.)
- Ritual Magic for Beginners (64 p.)
- Magic Chant for Beginners (108 p.)
- Invocations for Beginners (52 p.)
- Evocations for Beginners (62 p.)
- Auto-Movement for Beginners (60 p.)
- Elves for Beginners (56 p.)
- Hypnosis for Beginners (56 p.)
- Love Magic for Beginners (52 p.)
- Money Magic for Beginners (60 p.)
- Magic Objects for Beginners (64 p.)

- Shamanism for Beginners (52 p.)
- Chakra-Magic for Beginners (148 p.)
- Language of the Moon – for Beginners (128 p.)
- Self Knowledge for Beginners (60 p.)
- Astrology for Beginners (112 p.)
- Number Symbolism for Beginners (64 p.)
- Mandalas for Beginners (76 p.)
- Crop Circles for Beginners (344 p.)
- Feng Shui for Beginners (96 p.)

These books will be puplished soon:

- Kundalini for Beginners
- Magic Research for Beginners
- Symbolism of Numbers for Beginners
- Da'ath-Magic for Beginners
- Magic for Beginners – Anthology I
- Magic for Beginners – Anthology II
- Magic for Beginners – Anthology III
- Magic for Beginners – Anthology IV

Bücher von Harry Eilenstein

Religion allgemein
- Die sieben Schritte des Lebens (428 S.)
- Muttergöttin und Schamanen (168 S.)
- Göbekli Tepe (472 S.)
- Die Göttin von Göbekli Tepe (144 S.)
- Die Biographie des Teufels (144 S.)
- Totempfähle (440 S.)
- Christus (60 S.)
- Dakini (80 S.)
- Vajra (76 S.)

Ägypten
- Hathor und Re 1: Götter und Mythen im Alten Ägypten (432 S.)
- Hathor und Re 2: Die altägyptische Religion – Ursprünge, Kult und Magie (396 S.)
- Isis (508 S.)

Indogermanen
- Die Entwicklung der indogermanischen Religionen (700 S.)
- Wurzeln und Zweige der indogermanischen Religion (224 S.)

Germanen
- Die Götter der Germanen (87 Bände – siehe nächste Seite)
- Odin (300 S.)

Kelten
- Cernunnos (690 S.)
- Taliesin (228 S.)
- Der Kessel von Gundestrup (220 S.)
- Der Chiemsee-Kessel (76)

Psychologie
- Über die Freude (100 S.)
- Das Geheimnis des inneren Friedens (252 S.)
- Das Beziehungsmandala (52 S.)
- Gefühle und ihre Verwandlungen (404 S.)
- einsgerichtet (140 S.)
- Liebe und Eigenständigkeit (216 S.)
- Von innerer Fülle zu äußerem Gedeihen (52 S.)

Heilung
- Die Symbolik der Krankheiten (76 S.)

Kunst
- Herz des Tanzes – Tanz des Herzens (160 S.)

Drama
- König Athelstan (104 S.)

Bücher von Harry Eilenstein

„Magie für Anfänger"	**Magie**

„Magie für Anfänger"

- Telepathie für Anfänger (60 S.)
- Telepathie für Fortgeschrittene (52 S.)
- Telekinese für Anfänger (52 S.)
- Lebenskraft für Anfänger (60 S.)
- Meditation für Anfänger (56 S.)
- Kundalini für Anfänger (100 S.)
- Hypnose für Anfänger (56 S.)
- Auto-Movement für Anfänger (56 S.)
- Chakra-Magie für Anfänger (148 S.)
- Astralreisen für Anfänger (56 S.)
- Astrologie für Anfänger (120 S.)
- Ritual-Magie für Anfänger (56 S.)
- Mandalas für Anfänger (68 S.)
- Geldzauber für Anfänger (56 S.)
- Liebeszauber für Anfänger (52 S.)
- Invokationen für Anfänger (52 S.)
- Evokationen für Anfänger (60 S.)
- Elfen für Anfänger (56 S.)
- Magie-Forschung für Anfänger (140 S.)
- Selbsterkenntnis für Anfänger (52 S.)
- Zahlensymbolik für Anfänger (60 S.)
- Die Sprache des Mondes – für Anfänger (116 S.)
- Zaubergesänge für Anfänger (100 S.)
- Zukunftschau für Anfänger (60 S.)
- Schamanismus für Anfänger (52 S.)
- Magische Gegenstände für Anfänger (68 S.)
- Da'ath-Magie für Anfänger (64 S.)
- Kornkreise für Anfänger (348 S.)
- Feng Shui für Anfänger (96 S.)
- Magie für Anfänger – Sammelband I (696 S.)
- Magie für Anfänger – Sammelband II (664 S.)
- Magie für Anfänger – Sammelband III (580 S.)

„Traumreisen"

- Traumreisen zu Heilpflanzen (700 S.)

Magie

- Handbuch für Zauberlehrlinge (408 S.)
- Tarot (104 S.)
- Physik und Magie (184 S.)
- Die Synthese von Physik und Magie (200S.)
- Die Magie-Formel (156 S.)
- Krafttiere – Tiergöttinnen – Tiertänze (112 S.)
- Schwitzhütten (524 S.)
- Mythen und Magie der Harfe (116 S.)
- Magie heute – Berichte aus der Praxis (288 S.)

Meditation

- Der Lebenskraftkörper (230 S.)
- Die Chakren (100 S.)
- Das Chakren-System mit den Nebenchakren (296 S.)
- Organe und Chakren (64 S.)
- Die platonischen Körper in den Chakren (156 S.)
- Meditation (140 S.)
- Drachenfeuer (124 S.)
- Kundalini I (676 S.)
- Reinkarnation (156 S.)
- einsgerichtet (140 S.)

Astrologie

- Astrologie (496 S.)
- Photo-Astrologie (428 S.)
- Die astrologischen Aspekte (88 S.)
- Horoskop und Seele (120 S.)

Kabbala

- Kursus der praktischen Kabbala (150 S.)
- Eltern der Erde (450 S.)
- Blüten des Lebensbaumes:
    - Die Struktur des kabbalistischen Lebensbaumes (370 S.)
    - Der kabbalistische Lebensbaum als Forschungshilfsmittel (580 S.)
    - Der kabbalistische Lebensbaum als spirituelle Landkarte (520 S.)

Die Themen der 87 Bände der Reihe „Die Götter der Germanen"